IN OUR OWN BACKYARD

Principles for
Effective Improvement
of the
Nation's Infrastructure

COMMITTEE ON INFRASTRUCTURE
BUILDING RESEARCH BOARD
COMMISSION ON ENGINEERING AND TECHNICAL SYSTEMS
NATIONAL RESEARCH COUNCIL

Albert A. Grant
Andrew C. Lemer
Editors

NATIONAL ACADEMY PRESS
WASHINGTON, D.C.
1993

Funding for the project was provided through the following agreements between the indicated federal agency and the National Academy of Sciences: Department of the Army Agreement CECWXX-90-N-5301 and DACA88-92-M-0283; Federal Highway Administration Agreement DTFH61-92-P-01352; and National Science Foundation Grant No. MSS-9009343, under master agreement 8618642.

Library of Congress Catalog Card Number 93-87112
International Standard Book Number 0-309-04878-8

Additional copies of this report are available from:
National Academy Press
2101 Constitution Avenue, NW
Box 285
Washington, D.C. 20055
800-624-6242 or 202-334-3313 (in the Washington Metropolitan Area)

B-134

COMMITTEE ON INFRASTRUCTURE

iii

RICHARD L. SIEGLE, P.E. Director of Facilities Services, Smithsonian Institution, Washington, D.C.

RAYMOND L. STERLING, Associate Professor and Director, Underground Space Center, University of Minnesota, Minneapolis

NAN STOCKHOLM, Director, Presidio Council, Golden Gate National Park Association, San Francisco, California

National Research Council Liaison Representatives

NANCY CONNERY, Consultant, Woolwich, Maine

Federal Liaison Representatives

KEN P. CHONG, National Science Foundation, Washington, D.C.

CHARLES W. NEISSNER, Federal Highway Administration, Reston, Virginia

KYLE SCHILLING, U.S. Army Corps of Engineers, Fort Belvoir, Virginia

ROBERT STEARNS, Department of the Army, Washington, D.C.

Staff

ANDREW C. LEMER, Staff Officer
PATRICIA M. WHOLEY, Staff Associate
SUZETTE CODY, Project Assistant
MARY McCORMACK, Project Assistant

Acknowledgements

The committee would like to acknowledge the assistance of the many people in Phoenix, Cincinnati, and Boston who guided and participated in this study. While many of these individuals are listed in the Appendixes of this report there were many others who provided invaluable services. In particular the committee would like to thank the American Public Works Association for providing meeting rooms, hotel and other logistical arrangements in Boston.

iv

WALTER P. MOORE, President and Chairman of the Board, Walter P. Moore and Associates, Inc., Houston, Texas

J. W. MORRIS, U.S.A. Retired, President, J. W. Morris Ltd., Arlington, Virginia

BRIAN P. MURPHY, Senior Vice President, Prudential Property Company, Prudential Plaza, Newark, New Jersey

LESLIE E. ROBERTSON*, Director, Design and Construction, Leslie E. Robertson Associates, New York, New York

JEROME J. SINCOFF, AIA, President, Hellmuth, Obata & Kassabaum, Inc., St. Louis, Missouri

JAMES E. WOODS*, William E. Jamerson Professor of Building Construction, College of Architecture and Urban Studies, Virginia Polytechnic Institute and State University, Blacksburg

APRIL L. YOUNG*, CRA Coordinator, First American Metro Corporation, McLean, Virginia

Staff

ANDREW C. LEMER, Director
HENRY A. BORGER, Executive Secretary, Federal Construction Council
PATRICIA M. WHOLEY, Staff Associate
SUZETTE CODY, Project Assistant
LENA B. GRAYSON, Program Assistant
MARY McCORMACK, Project Assistant

---

*Term completed

CONTENTS

EXECUTIVE SUMMARY 1

1.   INTRODUCTION 13

What the Report Contains, 15
Thinking Broadly, Observing Locally, 16

2.   THINKING BROADLY ABOUT INFRASTRUCTURE 19

Infrastructure's Many Services, 20
Public Works and Private, 23
Evolving Technologies, 24
Institutions and Infrastructure, 31

3.   OBSERVING LOCALLY 37

The Colloquia Series, 37
Phoenix, Arizona, 41
    Background, 41
    Asphalt Pavement Using Recycled Rubber Tires and
      Other Design Features, 45
    Papago Freeway and Margaret Hance Park, 47
    Squaw Peak Parkway and Thomas Road Overpass, 48
    27th Avenue Solid Waste Management Facility, 51
    Water Resources and Canals, 52
    Grass-Roots Initiative and Sunnyslope Village, 55
    How Representative Is the Phoenix Experience?, 56
    Extracting More General Principles, 58

Cincinnati, Ohio, 60
    Background, 60
    The Stormwater Management Utility, 62

The Infrastructure Commission, 65
The Infrastructure Improvement Program, 69
How Representative Is the Cincinnati Experience?, 72
Extracting More General Principles, 74

Boston, Massachusetts, 76
Background, 76
Public Transport, Public Involvement, and the
Southwest Corridor, 78
Building the Central Artery/Third Harbor Tunnel, 81
Massachusetts Water Resource Authority "Turning the
Tide on Pollution," 83
How Representative Is the Boston Experience?, 85
Extracting More General Principles, 87

4.   PRINCIPLES FOR ACTION ON INFRASTRUCTURE 89

Three Key Principles for Action, 90
Principle 1: Geography Matters, 90
Principle 2: The Paradigm Is Broadening, 92
Principle 3: Value the "Public" in Public Works, 94
Toward National Policy and Beyond, 98

APPENDIXES

A. Biographical Sketches of Committee Members and Staff, 103
B. The BRB/CETS/NRC Strategic Program in Infrastructure, 108
C. Study Participants, 113

List of Tables

Table 3-1 Summary Statistics on Workshop Cities, 42, 43

List of Pictures

1-A. Many elements of the infrastructure interact underground, hidden from view. Here water supply pipelines surface and are supported by a bridge across a concrete-lined stormwater drainage channel that replaced a creek, 18.

2-A.   Cincinnati's cable suspension bridge across the Ohio River continues to carry traffic more than 100 years after its construction. The bridge, in 1866 America's longest span, was designed by John Roebling, whose technical achievement and artistry in the Brooklyn Bridge established him as one of the most famous of America's infrastructure professionals, 29.

3-A.   By questioning the state's standard bridge design originally planned for the Thomas Road Overpass, part of the Squaw Peak Parkway in Phoenix, the artist invited to "beautify" an austere structure motivated a money-saving custom design and created an award-winning community asset, 49.

3-B.   The engineer-artist team responsible for design of Phoenix's 27th Avenue Solid Waste Management Facility, here under construction, created an entry to the building that would illustrate to the public something about how structures work, 53.

3-C.   Accumulated "superficial" deterioration and subsequent structural damage on Cincinnati's Ludlow Viaduct were a direct result of the neglect of maintenance, attributable to legislative budgetary decisions. Until repairs could be made, the bridge had to be closed to truck traffic, adding substantially to street congestion and the costs to businesses located in the area, 66.

3-D.   Cincinnati's Ault Park Pavilion was renovated in 1992 and returned to service as a popular place for strolling and a center for community recreation. Parks, open space, and such public facilities are likely to become increasingly important as elements of infrastructure, 73.

3-E.   This approach to downtown Boston—lined with houses and small shops, and passing through flower and vegetable gardens, parks and playgrounds—is built above the Metropolitan Boston Transportation Authority's Orange Line. Much of the rapid rail transit line is, in turn, located in a right of way cleared in the 1960s for construction of a segment of the interstate highway system. Community questioning of the balance and distribution of costs and benefits of this segment led to the nation's first major reprogramming of federal transportation funds from one mode to another, 80.

3-F.   Infrastructure construction projects are often among the largest and most complex and costly civil engineering undertakings. Operations of this dredge working on Boston's Third Harbor Tunnel project adjust to seasonal fish migrations as well as tides and storms, 86.

4-A.   In Boston's South End neighborhood, matching the design of the subway transit's ventilation tower to the style of adjacent residences converted a potential eyesore and source of community resentment to an attractive and accepted addition to the urban landscape, 96.

EXECUTIVE SUMMARY

The nation's infrastructure has become a steady theme of national debate and almost a household word. As a source for new jobs in a slow-growth economy, a means for better protection of the environment, an instrument for community development, or an ingredient in restoring America's global competitive strength, infrastructure has come increasingly to be seen as a major part of the solution to pressing national problems. At the same time, infrastructure collapse and destruction—in Chicago's tunnels, Washington's power supply, or New York's steam lines; in Florida's hurricane or California's earthquake—are reminders of how fragile the system may be and how dependent we are on the services of infrastructure.

Infrastructure's emergence from technical obscurity follows more than a decade of study and debate. Representing a total investment that may exceed $1.4 trillion, the nation's infrastructure is said by many people to be "in ruins." Many policy makers and members of the public have expressed understandable skepticism when presented with such dire assessments. They observe that failures are isolated, primarily in a few older cities, and many elements of the nation's infrastructure seemingly continue to work quite well. While some communities find that the pinch of tight budgets constrains their ability to maintain what they have, others willingly vote to approve bond issues or other means to pay for refurbishing aging facilities or building new ones.

Nevertheless, even those who question the extreme views of the status of U.S. infrastructure have come to recognize that **problems do exist**. Technological and institutional complexity

1

inhibits both coordinated action and discussion of the cross-cutting issues of infrastructure and its technological advancement.

A National Research Council committee, drawing on its members' experience and observations in cities around the country, spent more than a year seeking to gain better understanding of these problems and how they might be solved. During the spring and summer of 1992, the committee held workshop colloquia in three communities—Phoenix, Arizona; Cincinnati, Ohio; and Boston, Massachusetts—selected from a longer list of candidates because they seemed to have experienced notable successes in uniting and mobilizing to come to grips with their infrastructure problems.

This report presents what the committee found and its recommendations for what should be done—by policy makers, infrastructure professionals, and the public at large—to improve the nation's infrastructure. These recommendations call for change in the ways we think about and manage our infrastructure.

A NEED FOR CHANGE

For the most part, infrastructure is built and operated locally and supports virtually all local economic and social activity. The committee's experience makes clear that **change must begin at the local level.**

The complexity and multifunctional nature of the facilities and services that comprise a region's infrastructure are poorly reflected in the system's management. In most regions, **the various modes of infrastructure (e.g., transportation, water supply, waste disposal) are managed separately,** with few effective ways of dealing with the trade-offs among modes. While each distinct mode provides uniquely important services, **infrastructure's diverse modes function as a system, providing supportive services to a wide range of economic and social activities, a crucial enabling environment for economic growth, and enhanced quality of life.**

Infrastructure facilities and services support neighborhoods and communities. The current and long-term costs of infrastructure, both monetary costs and adverse impacts, are not borne equally by those who benefit from infrastructure's services. Adverse impacts (such as neighborhood disruption or air pollution) of infrastructure may extend well beyond a facility's immediate users and neighbors.

The policies and management practices typically shaping a region's infrastructure are a product of decades of growth and investment. These policies and practices emphasize the design and construction of facilities, and **deal poorly with operating efficiencies, the services infrastructure provides to the public, the unwanted by-products of infrastructure, and the imperatives of maintenance.** Operating and maintenance procedures, management practices, and development policies (i.e., infrastructure's software) are essential elements of the system. **Software and hardware must work together** and with societal demands to produce effective infrastructure performance. Infrastructure professionals must be prepared to deal effectively with this software.

The nation's economy is a product of its many local regions, and national policy influences local infrastructure, often profoundly. National inefficiencies and inequities that could be tolerated in times of rapid growth have become burdensome as the nation seeks to define sustainable futures.

Despite the infrastructure system's crucial importance for the nation's economy and quality of life, there is no national center of responsibility for infrastructure policy, nor is there a clearly delineated statement of such policy, although several federal agencies have independent roles in the development or regulation of specific modes. At the same time, new technologies offer opportunities for greatly enhanced service, but the relative inflexibility of the current system inhibits their development and adoption. New legislation such as the Intermodal Surface Transportation Efficiency Act (ISTEA) of 1991 offers hope for change, but more is needed. **National infrastructure policy must shift toward a more broadly defined, more integrated, and more locally tailored approach to infrastructure.**

BUILDING ON EXPERIENCE

The committee's workshops in Phoenix, Cincinnati, and Boston highlighted how a city's location, history, economy, and culture influence its infrastructure and are influenced by it. The locally focused, cross-modal and service-oriented perspective of this study marked an important departure from most earlier work. The committee observed that **communities working together can make progress in dealing with the problems of infrastructure,** but it takes time, patience, imagination, and a willingness to devote resources to the task.

The infrastructure of **Phoenix,** a city "at the threshold of maturity," is a product of a desert setting, rapid growth driven in part by major infrastructure investments, low-density urbanization, and large areas of open space. The modern settlement of Phoenix began in the late 1860s, but bears the mark of ancient native people who built canals and roads several centuries before this modern growth.

In Phoenix, the committee found an infrastructure shaped by a unique coalition of the arts and public works communities. This coalition appears to have fostered imaginative ways of dealing with community concerns and has enhanced the levels of communication and trust between infrastructure professionals and the public at large. The coalition's work is reflected in newly developed highway and solid waste management facilities. The committee also found technological innovation in locally developed processes for using ground rubber, from waste vehicular tires, as an asphalt additive to improve overlay adhesion and hot-weather perfor- mance. The new mix is said to have superior working characteris- tics and physical behavior; it resists bleaching in the Arizona sun and results in a 10-decibel reduction in tire-pavement noise, com- pared to conventional pavements. The city, now using rubber from approximately 300,000 recycled tires annually, pays no li- cense fees for using the process. The city engineer who was given the opportunity to innovate was well rewarded for his efforts.

Cincinnati is a mature city, founded shortly after the American Revolution and built on steep hills and bluffs overlooking the Ohio

4

River and tributaries. Present-day Cincinnati has a relatively compact downtown area and some 25 miles of municipally owned retaining walls, more than any other city in the United States.

In the mid-1980s, the city was a victim of a classic crisis of declining population and tax base and aging facilities, a crisis it faced through a concerted effort of its infrastructure professionals and its business community. This coalition worked to inform the public of infrastructure's importance to the community's prosperity and then to mobilize community resources to pay for the increased spending required both to "catch up" with past deficiencies and to maintain the city's infrastructure in the future. The centerpiece of this effort was the Infrastructure Commission, a small group of volunteer leaders of the business community who, in turn, recruited the participation of almost 200 other volunteers from throughout the business community.

These volunteers worked with city staff, contributing more than 10,000 person-hours over the course of one year to assess the city's infrastructure and make recommendations for bringing the city's physical assets back to good condition and appearance. The commission developed a comprehensive package of specific recommendations for facilities and operating improvements, and for funding to enable the increased levels of spending required to implement these improvements. A substantial share of the needed revenue came from an increase in the city's earnings tax, narrowly approved by the voters in a 1988 referendum.

Boston, the oldest and most historic of the three cities visited by the committee, has demonstrated over the years a historic inclination of its citizens to consider bold civic visions and set the city on a course to remake itself, while seeking to preserve its most important historic landmarks. Today, Boston is in the midst of a major cycle of refurbishment and expansion of its infrastructure that includes new rail transit lines, as well as highway and sewage treatment projects of monumental proportions.

These major projects bring to the forefront the questions of national interests in local infrastructure, through their large scale and their use of national resources—in some cases financial, in other cases judicial and administrative. The estimated combined cost of the two ongoing projects, the Central Artery/Third Harbor Tunnel and the Harbor Cleanup, is around $14 billion. Whether other technologies might be more effective or less costly is a matter of continuing debate. Maintaining timely progress and community support on such major projects presents truly major management challenges.

PRINCIPLES FOR SEEKING "WIN-WIN" OUTCOMES

In their visits to Phoenix, Cincinnati, and Boston, committee members talked to private citizens and representatives of the business communities and governments, who were grappling with issues of infrastructure development and management. From this experience, the committee extracted three broad principles for dealing with local infrastructure issues, principles that can lead toward "win-win" situations, in which parties with potentially opposing interests seek a way to resolve a conflict such that all parties gain. The committee observed specific examples in Boston, Cincinnati, and Phoenix that support and demonstrate these principles.

At their core, these principles represent a prescription for what works: good planning, good management, and good community relations. Within the context of practices of the past several decades, applying these principles means a shift toward a broader view and broader participation in the infrastructure.

The committee recommends these principles for policy makers, infrastructure professionals, and the public in communities facing infrastructure problems or simply seeking to enhance their ability to develop and manage more effectively. Ultimately this means all communities throughout the nation. The committee recommends that responsible government agencies and the Congress act to enable and encourage broad adoption of these principles in managing the nation's infrastructure.

Principle 1: Geography Matters

The specific physical, social, economic, and environmental characteristics of a region should be the primary factors shaping that region's infrastructure investment and management. National policy must deal effectively with local concerns, allowing solutions to be tailored to natural environment, social patterns, and locally assessed needs and aspirations of the region.

Cincinnati's need for retaining walls and the recurrent flooding in some neighborhoods are reminders that infrastructure should be designed and managed to **respect the natural features** (e.g., drainage, geology) and social structure of the community and to be compatible with these features. The history of Boston's transit extensions, converted from planned highways through intense community involvement, shows that there should be **respect** for **the social and cultural character of a region,** as well as compatibility. These **natural, social, and cultural features are connected** in complex ways that should shape the region's infrastructure.

To apply this principle effectively, local authorities must **collect and maintain good data** to support effective decision making **and good documentation** of the bases and consequences of decisions. Increasingly powerful and lower- cost computer-based geographic information systems will facilitate data management and documentation.

Principle 2: The Paradigm is Broadening

The pattern of infrastructure management must change from uncoordinated functional subsystems to incorporate a new recognition that infrastructure is a multimodal and multipurpose system—a stream of services—as well as an armature of community development. Phoenix's solid waste transfer facility—a product of artists and engineers collaborating in design—demonstrates this broader paradigm, that infrastructure facility planning, design, and management can seek to **deliver multiple services.** Boston's decades-long transportation system development shows how communities can **be flexible in allocating resources within the whole system to suit local conditions**, always examining multiple solutions for each problem and taking a long-term perspective in decision making, extending beyond the traditional 15- to 30-year design service life or bond financing horizon.

Increasing the investment in infrastructure, although often necessary and appropriate, is not sufficient by itself to solve a region's or the nation's problems. As Cincinnati's Infrastructure Commission found when faced with the task of assessing the city's problems, **new systems for monitoring and maintaining infrastructure condition and performance at appropriate levels are needed**, systems that are less susceptible to shifting political forces.

To the extent that national policies support infrastructure, these policies should be shifted from a narrow focus on transportation, water resources, or other single elements of the infrastructure system. **National infrastructure policies and programs should be structured to foster a new paradigm that applies across infrastructure modes and brings together the interests of diverse regions within a context of equity among cities and regions.**

This new paradigm must be presented and refined through education of infrastructure professionals and policy makers. **Infrastructure professionals need a broader and more integrative educational experience** that will enable them to communicate effectively with the public and policy makers, as well as manage the infrastructure system. The case of the Phoenix city engineer— who improved street pavement performance, saved the city money, and was himself well compensated for developing a way to use old tires in the asphalt concrete mix—demonstrates why policy makers should **give greater recognition to the enabling value of infrastructure, by promoting and rewarding innovation in infrastructure technology and management.**

Research and development contribute to our understanding of the services that infrastructure can provide and the options for providing these services more effectively, and may lead to innovation if results are transferred into practice. **Local** demonstrations are a valuable form of research and development that should be used to verify and disseminate new technology.

Principle 3: Value the "Public" in Public Works

Infrastructure serves the public, and effective public involvement and broad intersectoral and interdisciplinary partnerships in infrastructure development and management are needed to apply the broader paradigm. As the hard-earned success of Cincinnati's Infrastructure Commission showed, inclusion by the community of broad representation of users and neighbors of infrastructure within these partnerships strengthens decision making.

All three cities visited by the committee showed that to build leadership and effectiveness, the people responsible for approving infrastructure development (i.e., voters) need to be better informed to judge matters of infrastructure technology and its impact on the economy, the environment, and the general quality of life. **Public education is an essential element of future infrastructure management.**

Infrastructure professionals should **include community peer review of plans and progress as a regular part of major infrastructure decisionmaking.** Such peer review is an effective means for building the new coalitions of diverse interest groups that the broader paradigm will bring.

STARTING IN OUR OWN BACKYARD

Making these principles effective will require vision and leadership at local and national levels. The committee recommends that responsible government agencies and the Congress act to enable and encourage their broad adoption by policy makers, infrastructure professionals, and the public in communities throughout the nation face infrastructure problems or seek simply to enhance their ability to develop and manage more effectively.

Adequate infrastructure is a crucial element of the national enabling environment needed for increasing productivity and improving the quality of life. Effective national policy can support that enabling environment by providing the framework for alleviating many of the problems our infrastructure faces.

A national perspective can bring together the interests of diverse regions, maintaining equity among cities and regions and the fostering of structures in local government to support the new management paradigm of infrastructure as a system of services. National infrastructure policy can address effectively—in a way that is not possible at local levels alone—the balance of resources applied among infrastructure modes and between infrastructure and other issues of national interest. However, today's complex and often conflicting and inefficient collection of laws, regulations, standards, and programs that address separately the various modes and their impacts must be changed.

The ISTEA legislation, which includes broad provisions for intermodal coordination and community planning, indicates that change is possible at the national level, but the ISTEA is only a transportation act with little, if any, consequence for water supply, sewerage, telecommunications, and other elements of infrastructure. If communities are to take an integrated, multimodal view in developing and managing their infrastructure, federal programs must be fully supportive.

A particularly important form of support is the federal funding of infrastructure research, development, and especially demonstration activities. Such agencies as the National Science Foundation, Department of Transportation, U.S. Army Corps of Engineers, and Environmental Protection Agency can and should foster cross-cutting research to improve local areas' practical capabilities for life cycle management, condition monitoring and performance assessment, and information and system management.

Nevertheless, infrastructure is essentially local, and local differences will always require specific variations in facilities, management systems, and funding patterns. A supportive national policy environment is needed, policy that responds to our increasing recognition of global interdependence and responsibilities, but strategies for addressing issues of infrastructure must be applied locally--to paraphrase the often-used phrase of resistance to infrastructure--in our own backyards.

1

INTRODUCTION

In 1988, the National Research Council (NRC) and other elements of the academy complex,[1] concerned by the slow progress of national debate on infrastructure, undertook a strategic program designed to foster a more effective national focus and to produce new policies and programs for infrastructure improvement. The Building Research Board (BRB) has taken responsibility for this program, and in 1991 it established the Committee on Infrastructure, whose work is reported here.[2]

For more than a decade, the status and future of the nation's infrastructure have been matters of concern and discussion. Once a subject of interest primarily to professionals and politicians, the term has emerged from obscurity to become almost a household word. As a source for new jobs in a slow-growth economy, a means for better protection of the environment, or an essential ingredient in restoring America's global competitive strength,

---

[1]The NRC; its constituent commissions, boards, and committees; and its parent bodies—the National Academy of Sciences, National Academy of Engineering, and Institute of Medicine—are often referred to as "the academy complex."

[2]Appendix A presents biographical sketches of the committee's members and staff. Appendix B gives a brief history of the BRB program.

rebuilding America's fragile foundations has become a recurring metaphor for investment and reinvestment in transportation systems, water supply networks, telecommunications, and waste treatment facilities that is increasingly seen as a major part of the solution to pressing national problems.

While infrastructure has become a symbol of hope for some, the sudden onset of infrastructure collapse and destruction have also drawn public attention. A tunnel in Chicago, a main water line and major electrical transformer and cable in the nation's capital, steam lines in New York, the aftermath of Florida's hurricane or California's earthquake—all are reminders of how fragile the system may be and how dependent we are on the services of infrastructure.

The public's investment in U.S. infrastructure is enormous. Many people say that these assets are "in ruins." However, many policy makers and members of the public express understandable skepticism when presented with such dire assessments. They observe that failures are isolated, primarily in a few older cities, and many elements of the nation's infrastructure seemingly continue to work quite well. Some communities face fiscal stringency and voter rebellion, but in other locales the voters approve bonds and other means to pay for refurbishing aging facilities or building new ones.

Nevertheless, even those who question the extreme views of the status of U.S. infrastructure have come to recognize that problems do exist. Facilities are aging and deteriorating. Population has shifted within and among urban areas, causing the demands for infrastructure to shift as well. Technological and institutional complexity inhibits both planning and action. Innovation, proceeding at such a rapid pace in many fields, seems to some observers to come slowly to infrastructure (e.g., NCPWI, 1988).

The committee spent more than a year seeking to gain better understanding of such problems and to determine how solutions might be found. During the spring and summer of 1992, the committee held workshop colloquia in three communities— Phoenix, Arizona; Cincinnati, Ohio; and Boston, Massachusetts— to observe the seemingly notable successes these communities have had in uniting and mobilizing to come to grips with their infrastructure problems. The local experience of these communities offers lessons for others and for the nation as a whole.

WHAT THE REPORT CONTAINS

This report presents what the committee found and its recommendations for what should be done—by policy makers, infrastructure professionals, and the public at large—to improve the nation's infrastructure. These lessons call for change in the ways we think about and manage our infrastructure.

Chapter 2 describes the background and basic principles that were the starting point for the committee's deliberations. This starting point is represented, for the most part, by a broad perspective and what many analysts term a "top-down" approach to thinking about infrastructure. However, in contrast to the more typical pattern of dealing separately with water supply, waste management, highways, and other distinct elements of infrastructure, this report and the study as a whole consider infrastructure as an institutionally complex, multifunctional system serving a broad range of economic and social activities. This whole-system point of view is most easily comprehended in cities, and this study focuses on urban infrastructure. Chapter 3 presents the core of this work, the committee's search, in the local experience of three communities, for effective principles and strategies for improving infrastructure. Phoenix, Cincinnati, and Boston, selected from a longer list of candidates, provided the committee with a "bottom-up" view of national infrastructure issues. The committee's specific observations and assessments of this experience are the principal basis for its subsequent recommendations.

These recommendations are presented in Chapter 4. The committee undertook to identify the common elements of local successes and to extract lessons that could give practitioners, policy makers, and the public at large better understanding and guidance in dealing with infrastructure. The result is three key principles likely to lead to win-win solutions to local infrastructure problems. The term "win-win," popularized from mathematical game theory, conveys the committee's conclusion that it is possible to resolve the major conflicts in infrastructure development and management in ways such that all parties can gain. Establishing conditions conducive to resolving these conflicts in communities throughout the nation is the basis for national policy as well as local infrastructure development and management.

This report and the committee's recommendations are limited by the cases that were investigated, and several important infrastructure issues have not been addressed. For example, some communities faced with the costs of providing infrastructure to support rapid growth have chosen to search for ways to control that growth, to limit the demand for infrastructure, or to impose fees to mitigate the fiscal impact of new public works construction. Other communities, faced with declining economic activity and populations, are choosing to retire infrastructure facilities that they can no longer afford to maintain. Storms, earthquakes, and other catastrophes have damaged or destroyed important system elements, forcing what remains to serve in unplanned ways. Such cases would be excellent subjects for future studies.

In addition, evidence suggests that the ways in which local governments are organized and empowered makes a difference in how effectively infrastructure problems are identified and solved. While historians and planners have studied such matters (e.g., Anderson, 1977; Platt, 1983), they were only touched on in this committee's work.

THINKING BROADLY, OBSERVING LOCALLY

The three principles discussed in Chapter 4 reflect the committee's firm belief that national policy must respond more effectively to the variety of local conditions, and that construction alone is unlikely to yield real and lasting relief from serious infrastructure problems. This belief was asserted early in the committee's study, as a key element of its approach to issues of infrastructure: **the**

problems of infrastructure are essentially local but nevertheless have national policy significance. As already noted, this focus on local levels, but cutting across all modes (e.g., highways, water supply, waste treatment) of infrastructure, marks an important departure from most earlier policy studies, which have dealt primarily with one or two related modes viewed on a national level. The committee sought instead to bridge the gap between local concerns and those of national policy that influence local action and national well-being. This gap is illustrated by the growing vocabulary of terms describing public response to infrastructure development proposals. First NIMBY (Not in My Back Yard!) became a widely popular acronym and then the name for the syndrome of resistance. More recently appearing terms include NOTE (Not over There Either!) and NIMTOO (Not in My Term of Office!) In the extreme, the stance of some citizens' groups extends to BANANA (Build Absolutely Nothing Anywhere, Anytime!) Such attitudes must be changed, along with the policies that spawned them.

The committee felt that its greatest contributions would be in identifying transferable lessons from local experience, lessons that could be applied in other regions, and in extracting from these lessons the principles of national policy that will support the transfer. With that premise, and set against the backdrop of the continuing broad national discussions of infrastructure, the committee decided to hold its series of three regional colloquia.

REFERENCES

Anderson, Alan D. 1977. The Origin and Resolution of an Urban Crisis: Baltimore, 1890-1930. Baltimore, M.D.: The Johns Hopkins University Press.
NCPWI (National Council on Public Works Improvement). 1988. Fragile Foundations: A Report on America's Public Works. Washington, D.C.: U.S. Government Printing Office.
Platt, Harold L. 1983. City Building in the New South: The Growth of Public Services in Houston, Texas, 1830–1910. Philadelphia: Temple University Press.

Figure 1-A

Many elements of the infrastructure interact underground, hidden from view. Here water supply pipelines surface and are supported by a bridge across a concrete-lined stormwater drainage channel that replaced a creek.

2

THINKING BROADLY ABOUT INFRASTRUCTURE

More than a decade ago, experts began to raise alarms about the status of the nation's infrastructure. An early assessment warned of "America in ruins," and a succession of national commissions and private researchers followed with reports describing declining investment, neglected maintenance, "hard choices" to be made, and a growing need to "deliver the goods."[3]

Interestingly, the debate has proceeded without clear agreement on what comprises "infrastructure." Speaking at subcommittee hearings in 1987, former Senator Stafford commented that "probably the word infrastructure means different things to different people."[4] The word was coined, according to many dictionaries, in the first half of the twentieth century to refer to

---

[3]See Peterson (1979-1981), Choate and Walter (1981); Congressional Budget Office (CBO, 1983), National Infrastructure Advisory Committee (NIAC, 1984), National Council on Public Works Improvement (NCPWI, 1988), and Office of Technology Assessment (OTA, 1991). The National Research Council, has also published previously in this area, Hanson, 1984, NRC, 1987, Ausubel and Herman, 1988.

[4]Subcommittee on Water Resources, Transportation, and Infrastructure, Committee on Environment and Public Works, October 21, 1987.

military installations. Some researchers trace its origin to Winston Churchill; others, to earlier sources.

Now defined (by Webster's dictionary) as an "underlying foundation or basic framework," infrastructure has come to connote a diverse collection of constructed facilities and associated services, ranging from airports to energy supply to landfills to wastewater treatment. Many of the facilities are built and operated by governments, and thus fall easily into the category of public works, but others are built or operated, in whole or in part, by private enterprise or joint public-private partnership. What we today consider infrastructure has traditionally been viewed as separate systems of constructed facilities, supporting such functions as supplying water, enabling travel, and controlling floods. Especially at the national level, programs that spurred the growth of highways, modern water supplies, urban transit systems, and other infrastructure elements have developed independently of one another. The roots of this management paradigm[5] lie in the nineteenth century, but today the challenge of coordination is staggering.

INFRASTRUCTURE'S MANY SERVICES

An earlier committee of the National Research Council, reporting on *Infrastructure for the 21st Century* (NRC, 1987), adopted the term "public works infrastructure" including

both specific functional modes--highways, streets, roads, and bridges; mass transit; airports and airways; water

---

[5]The term "paradigm" has special significance in the context of this study. Historian of science Thomas Kuhn suggests that "the study of paradigms is what mainly prepares the student for membership in the particular scientific community with which he will later practice. Because he there joins men who learned the bases of their field from the same concrete models, his subsequent practice will seldom evoke overt disagreement over fundamentals. The transition to a new paradigm is scientific revolution" (Kuhn, 1970).

supply and water resources; wastewater management; solid-waste treatment and disposal; electric power generation and transmission; telecommunications; and hazardous waste management--and the combined system these modal elements comprise. A comprehension of infrastructure spans not only these public works facilities, but also the operating procedures, management practices, and development policies that interact together with societal demand and the physical world to facilitate the transport of people and goods, provision of water for drinking and a variety of other uses, safe disposal of society's waste products, provision of energy where it is needed, and transmission of information within and between communities.

To the specific modes cited in that description should be added systems of public buildings—schools, health care facilities, government offices, and the like. These facilities—not as individual buildings, but tied together by the functional and administrative systems they house—provide important services to the public at large, in much the same fashion as highways and water supply facilities (see Henning et al., 1991, for example).

Parkland, open space, urban forests, drainage channels and aquifers, and other hydrologic features also qualify as infrastructure, not only for their aesthetic and recreational value, but because they play important roles in supplying clean air and water. Even when they are not used directly as part of the supply system, such elements influence the demand for other infrastructure services. The modes are becoming increasingly important as we increase our efforts to avoid or mitigate an expanding list of environmental problems.

Viewed historically, new modes may enter the definition of infrastructure from time to time and others disappear. For example, walls and other fortifications were an important element of medieval city infrastructure, long before telephones were invented.

Studies done in the early 1970s for the U.S. Council for Environmental Quality estimated the per capita costs of infrastructure investment in typical U.S. mixed-density communities to be $1,500 to $2,000 (RERC, 1974). The 1992 figure is probably closer to $4,500 per capita, on average, and substantially higher in older, denser urban areas. BRB staff estimate that our infrastructure may represent a total national investment exceeding $1.4 trillion.

Operating and maintenance procedures, management practices, and development policies (i.e., the software) are also essential elements of infrastructure. **Software and hardware must work together to produce effective infrastructure performance.**

The various facilities of infrastructure ("infrastructures," as some term them, hardware and software) comprise the hard core of the concept, but **to discuss infrastructure only in terms of facilities neglects the important services provided by both private enterprise and public agencies, that are enabled by these facilities.** The creation and distribution of these infrastructure services occur through distinct economic and social actions that are influenced by many factors beyond the facilities themselves. Airlines and departments of education may be encouraged or constrained by their systems of airports and schoolhouses, but have broad latitude to adjust their operations and costs in response to demands.

These services are broadly important: public health and welfare, economic productivity, and individual quality of life depend essentially on infrastructure. The importance of transport access, telecommunications, or ample supplies of clean water to individual industries and cities is readily apparent. However, it is **the multimodal system of infrastructure as a whole that provides a crucial enabling environment for economic growth and enhanced quality of life.** This synergistic effect is most easily seen in the world's great cities, which could not have developed without infrastructure's support.

The beginning of Rome's water supply by Appius Claudius in 312 B.C. was an early step in the development of an infrastructure—which by the first century A.D. included paved roads, fire protection, and sewerage—that supported the city's centuries of undisputed dominance. Henry IV and his minister

Sully created the basis for several generations of France's prosperity by developing that nation's canals and roads. Advancing transportation technologies enabled the growth of the great industrial cities of the nineteenth century. In the current information age, electronic communications have become an important element of infrastructure, and cities from New York to Osaka seek to gain access by constructing "teleports" linking their businesses to the global satellite network.

In cities, the debilitating impact of inadequate infrastructure is notable as well. Production costs for goods and services are estimated to be as much as 30 percent higher in some cities of the developing world because firms must provide their own water and power supplies (Lee et al., 1986). Low economic productivity and high rates of morbidity and mortality, particularly among the young, are endemic results of poor water supplies, roads, and waste management, as well as other infrastructure deficiencies, in less developed nations.

At national levels, Aschauer (1989) attributed a major share of the decline in U.S. productivity since the 1960s to deficiencies in infrastructure investment, generating intense debate among economists. Others have found similar, if smaller, effects in regions of the United States (Munnell, 1990) and in countries at various stages of development (Khan, 1987). Reliable estimates of the aggregate productivity of infrastructure capital remain clouded by the complexities of data and competing explanations of cause.

PUBLIC WORKS AND PRIVATE

Within this broad view of infrastructure, "public works" are a focus of political debate in the 1990s, even to the extent of the 1992 presidential campaign. Defined by the American Public Works Association as "the physical structures and facilities developed or acquired by public agencies to house governmental functions and provide water, waste disposal, power, transportation and similar services to facilitate achievement of common social and economic objectives," **public works are the primary focus of this study. However, public works are infrastructure and thus include services as well as facilities, private as well as public aspects of their provision and management, and the broad range of "social and economic objectives" that infrastructure facilitates.**

Government and private sector operations can (and in many cities do) compete directly for the right to collect and dispose of municipal solid waste. The success of such corporations as Federal Express and DHL in air parcel delivery, for example, reflects the development of new private infrastructure services based on existing public infrastructures.

The national infrastructure debate of the last decade has been shaped by a variety of economic, social, and environmental forces that sometimes raise obstacles and at other times present opportunities to both private and public providers of infrastructure. The influences of technological change and society's corresponding shifts in concerns and priorities have been reflected in regulatory practices, government budgets, and patterns of private demand for infrastructure. Lack of coordination—and sometimes overt antagonism—among national, state, and local governments, among infrastructure modes; and between private and public providers of infrastructure has influenced and often retarded decisionmaking and action.

EVOLVING TECHNOLOGIES

Much of today's infrastructure relies on technologies that emerged initially in the nineteenth century. Brooklyn's (New York) was the first modern urban sewage treatment system, built in 1857 (Herman and Ausubel, 1988). The first concrete roads followed within two decades the 1824 invention of Portland cement, and the Place de la Concorde in Paris was paved with asphalt as early as 1835 (Hamilton, 1975). Modern water supply was born in London in the middle of the century. Alexander

Graham Bell invented the telephone in 1876, and Edison his electric light in 1880.

Evidence shows that there is a relatively long time period, on the order of 100 years in the case of rail and road, in the transition from one infrastructure technology to the next (Grubler, 1990). The overall character of today's water supply and sewerage systems would be recognizable to an engineer of the nineteenth century, although the chemicals and controls used in processing have evolved substantially. The middle part of the nineteenth century was a highly productive period for infrastructure technology, a result of the convergence of new invention with rapid expansion of investment as the Industrial Revolution spread and America moved west. The rapid growth of railways in England demonstrates a concurrence of two technologies (i.e., the iron wagonway and the steam engine) that enabled this mode of transport to develop, just as in a later century a quantum leap in road transport performance became possible after introduction of the internal combustion engine. Before that, even ambitious road construction programs could not significantly improve the slow transport speeds of horse-drawn carriages and wagons (Grubler, 1990).

Change in infrastructure technologies, despite such evidence, can be more rapid. Electric power generating plants, for example, have been expected to last only 25 to 30 years. These facilities have typically become noncompetitive within this time frame, as newer more efficient equipment is introduced (Marland and Weinberg, 1988). Currently, that perception is said to be changing—and lifetimes are lengthening—as designers reach the ceiling of thermodynamic efficiency in conventional generation technology, but new technologies offering higher efficiencies (such as gas turbine or integrated gasification combined cycle processes (White et al., 1992) are on the horizon. In telecommunications as well, obsolescence currently is more likely than wear or other deterioration to motivate replacement of equipment.

Changes in technologies typically respond to demands for goods and services. With infrastructure, the demand is often complex, derived from the support it provides for other social and economic activities. Generally speaking, greater numbers of people and higher levels of economic activity mean greater demand for infrastructure. However, as rush-hour highway commuters and airport users frequently observe firsthand, the performance and capacity of infrastructures are acutely sensitive to patterns in time and space, as well as to the overall magnitude of underlying demand. The number of people who experience severe congestion and delays during a peak period could be easily accommodated with high-quality service if their travel were more evenly distributed throughout the day. The engineering design of an airport passenger terminal, for example, is typically based on peak demand levels that are 50 to 150 percent greater than would be needed if demand were spread evenly over time, and the factor can be even greater in other elements of infrastructure.

Most infrastructures are linked in networks. Roads and interchanges; water treatment plants, supply mains, and distributors; generating plants, transmission lines, and step-down transformers; sewers, treatment plants, and outfalls—all are tied tightly to one another and to thousands of individual households and businesses. These networks stretch over large areas and quickly transmit changes from one part of the system to another, and the functions of the whole surpass the sum of the parts. Thus, when one transmission line crossing the Potomac River failed one afternoon early in 1992, downtown Washington, D.C., was plunged into total darkness. The breaching of a segment of a disused tunnel in Chicago, some weeks later, caused the flooding of much of the Windy City's downtown. One minor accident on an urban highway can cause miles-long traffic jams during rush hour.

Because of large facility size and network extent, infrastructure often has broad environmental and social impacts, but these impacts frequently have been underestimated or neglected in system planning and management. For example, congested roads in 39 U.S. cities are estimated to have cost drivers more than $34 billion in 1988, in delays, wasted fuel, and higher insurance premiums (Hanks and Lomax, 1990). In another study, air pollution from motor vehicles was found to be responsible for $40 billion to 50 billion in annual healthcare expenditures and as many as 120,000 unnecessary or premature deaths (Cannon, 1989). Such costs, seldom considered by agencies deciding whether to invest in highways or transit, add perhaps $0.07 per mile to the costs paid by individuals choosing to travel by private auto.[6]

Institutionalization of environmental concerns in legislation, regulation, and formalization of impact assessment and planning procedures has increased the time and cost of the various steps required before any major action concerning infrastructure can be taken. A rapid expansion of U.S. environmental legislation in recent years has resulted in an "uncoordinated patchwork" of control requirements that has grown, by one count, from only 7 environmental laws enacted in the entire history of the United States until 1955 to more than 40 by 1986 (Balzhiser, 1989). These laws, a reflection of important societal priorities, have slowed and sometimes stopped investments or introductions of technology in infrastructure that would have been accomplished easily in prior decades. However, a valuable consequence is the emerging shift toward environmentally beneficial technologies, more supportive of "sustainable" economic and social activity.

Infrastructure is generally capital intensive. Because of high initial costs, the commissioning of a new dam, treatment plant, or highway is often a newsworthy event that attracts public attention. The costs of regular maintenance and operations seem small compared to construction but may, over the course of a facility's service life, total much more than the facility's initial costs. Infrastructure managers and elected officials, faced with the challenge of balancing competing public priorities and limited fiscal resources, often find it easy to defer maintenance spending and neglect infrastructure's upkeep. Unfortunately, deferrals speed deterioration and failures of the infrastructure. In sub-Saharan Africa, for example, the problem has reached extreme levels. The World Bank estimated that the backlog of neglected maintenance for roads alone exceeds $5 billion, more than seven times the

---

[6]Committee staff estimate, based on distributions of U.S. vehicle and highway mileage.

annual spending needed to keep the roads in good shape (World Bank, 1989).

Nevertheless, infrastructures are expected to be long-lived and are routinely designed to meet demands projected for three decades or more into the future. Most dams, bridges, highways, and other infrastructures endure much longer. For example the Brooklyn Bridge is still performing well after more than 100 years; the Alicante Dam has survived nearly four centuries; and such cities as Venice, Paris, and London have functioning facilities that are much older.[7] Facilities are in many instances taken out of service only because a competing one can perform the service more effectively or because the service is no longer particularly valuable—for example, a bridge is too narrow for increased traffic loads. These long capital investment cycles and facility lifetimes retard the adoption of newer and potentially more productive technologies.

During the time between major investments, governments (as the primary builders of infrastructure's facilities) and the populations they serve grow comfortable with patterns of spending that often include no allowance for depreciation or replacement of capital. Government accounting standards lack measures of financial condition equivalent to the private corporation's balance sheet. Attention to substantial public assets and consequent investment spending are episodic, making opportunities for change or the application of new technologies rare in any particular city or region.

Looking to such common characteristics, the Office of Technology Assessment highlighted five major areas of cross-cutting technology that offer opportunities for improving infrastructure (OTA, 1991):[8]

---

[7]Of course, long life is not ensured: the Grand Teton Dam failed immediately when the reservoir was filled, and the Takoma Narrows Bridge, famous for its unexpected dynamic response to winds, collapsed four months after its opening.

[8]Others have made similar assessments. The BRB is conducting a study, scheduled for completion by early 1994, to recommend an infrastructure research agenda for the National Science Foundation.

Figure 2-A

Cincinnati's cable suspension bridge across the Ohio River continues to carry traffic more than 100 years after its construction. The bridge, in 1866 America's longest span, was designed by John Roebling, whose technical achievement and artistry in the Brooklyn Bridge established him as one of the most famous of America's infrastructure professionals.

- *Measurement and non-destructive evaluation tools* will enable infrastructure managers to survey the condition of large structures and extensive networks of pipe and pavement, quickly and without inflicting additional damage.
- *Information and decision systems* will permit monitoring of use and resource scheduling to concentrate management effort where it will be most effective.
- *Communications and positioning systems* will facilitate control of geographically distributed infrastructure systems and improve the systemwide delivery of service to users.
- *Field construction technologies* will enhance the efficiency and safety of facility construction and rehabilitation.
- *Materials and corrosion* protection improvements will offer higher strength, longer life, and hence greater efficiencies in future infrastructure.

These five areas are not new. Rather, they represent incremental improvement of existing and sometimes widely used technology. Their value is nevertheless substantial, particularly because incremental improvements are more easily put into practice.

Some professionals feel that major breakthroughs in new technology are potentially available as well. Alternative systems involving new concepts or technologies could replace today's infrastructure systems (NRC, 1987). For example, riboflavin (also known as vitamin B_2) has been found to accelerate sunlight's ability to break down certain industrial pollutants in wastewater, foreshadowing perhaps substantially improved waste treatment efficiencies. Genetically engineered algae and bacteria could allow sewage treatment to begin at the source—possibly in tanks located next to the hot-water reservoir in homes and commercial facilities—reducing the load on central municipal plants.

However, societal concern about technological risk has grown significantly over recent years in the United States and elsewhere. This growth is a result of the increasing complexity of infrastructure technology and perceived increases in the potentially adverse consequences of making a mistake. These factors are poorly understood by the general population. Individuals sometimes fear they may be exposed not only to undesirable environmental conditions (e.g., noise, division of the neighborhood, consequent loss of property value), but also to unforeseen hazards to health and safety (e.g., toxic substances, electromagnetic radiation, heavy vehicular traffic). Peoples' concern about potential risk is increased when the cause of risk is perceived as particularly dread (e.g., cancer), uncontrollable (e.g., nuclear explosion), or of unknown proportion (Slovic et al., 1985). These concerns inevitably shape the course of infrastructure's technological evolution.

INSTITUTIONS AND INFRASTRUCTURE

The evolution of infrastructure occurs within a context of established institutions and interests, and most cities and their regions lack an effective mechanism for planning and management of infrastructure as a whole system. A myriad of local, regional, and national government agencies, quasi-governmental institutions, and private firms typically are involved in the planning, creation, operation, and regulation of physical infrastructure. The jurisdictions of these various bodies may be defined by political boundaries, historic precedent, or institutional competition that has little to do with the topography, demographics, or other features of the region that influence system performance and might provide a logical basis for efficient management.

This institutional complexity inhibits both coordinated action and discussion of the cross-cutting issues of infrastructure and its technological advancement. Further, despite the crucial importance of infrastructure for the nation's economy and quality of life, there is no federal center of responsibility for infrastructure policy. Instead responsibility is distributed among several federal agencies that have independent roles in the development or regulation of specific modes such as transportation, energy supply and transport, telecommunications, and water resources.

In fact, throughout the national debate, there has been little agreement on the nature of infrastructure and even less agreement that common action is warranted. Engineering and public administration professions tend to deal independently with transportation, water supply, or waste management, and give relatively little attention to the common features or functional interactions of these separate systems. Ever since the initial claims of a system in ruins, many policy makers and members of the public have expressed understandable skepticism, observing that despite pessimistic projections, many elements of the nation's infrastructure seemingly continue to work well. These skeptics assert that aggregate trends have little practical meaning; actual needs are limited to a few facilities and concentrated in a few geographic areas. While some communities feel the pinch of tight budgets, in many others the public willingly votes to approve bond issues or other means to pay for refurbishing aging facilities or building new ones (e.g., see Sanders, 1991).

An obstacle to effective national action is bridging the gap between national policy and diverse local concerns. Studies to date have largely neglected infrastructure's local "users," including those people who may view particular infrastructures as a burden out of proportion to their local benefit. This neglect is manifest in the widespread NIMBY (Not in My Backyard) and similar responses to infrastructure projects.

Conflict develops between some groups of people—typically defined by a particular locality or other community character-istics—and the more general community at large. Members of the former see themselves as potential "losers" in the conflict because they are asked to bear what they view as adverse impact out of proportion to the benefit they receive. A neighborhood will then resist improvement of streets in the area out of fear that the traffic of commuters riding through the neighborhood will increase. A small town will object to the siting of a solid waste transfer facility that will enhance the efficiency of the regional waste management system. A community will fight its destruction and replacement by major highways and urban redevelopment.

Against this background of limited agreement, technological obstacles, and institutional complexity, the nation's difficulties in dealing effectively with its infrastructure problems are not surprising. However, progress has been made in local areas here and there around the country. The committee sought to observe the characteristics of, and bases for, the progress and to extract lessons for the nation.

REFERENCES

Aschauer, D. 1989. The macroeconomic importance of public capital. Presented at a colloquium: The Role of Infrastructure in America's Economy, sponsored by Financial Guaranty Insurance Company and the Public's Capital, Washington, D.C.

Ausubel, J.H. and R. Herman, eds. 1988. Cities and Their Vital Systems: Infrastructure Past, Present, and Future. Washington, D.C.: National Academy Press.

Balzhizer, R.E. 1989. Meeting the near term challenge for power plants. In Technology and Environment, J.S. Ausubel and H.E. Sladovich, eds. Washington, D.C.: National Academy Press.

Cannon, J.S. 1989. The Health Costs of Air Pollution: A Survey of Studies Published 1984-1989. New York: American Lung Association.

CBO (U.S. Congress, Congressional Budget Office). 1983. Public Works Infrastructure: Policy Considerations for the 1980's. Washington, D.C.: U.S. Government Printing Office.

Choate, P., and S. Walter. 1981. America in Ruins: Beyond the Public Works Pork Barrel. Washington, D.C.: Council of State Planning Agencies.

Grubler, A. 1990. The Rise and Fall of Infrastructures: Dynamics of Evolution and Technological Change in Transport. Heidelberg: Physica-Verlag.

Hamilton, S.B. 1975. Building and civil engineering construction. In A History of Technology, Vol. IV: The Industrial

Revolution c 1750 to c 1850, C. Singer et al., eds. Oxford, Clarendon Press.

Hanks, J.W., Jr., and T.J. Lomax. 1990. Roadway Congestion in Major Urban Areas 1982 to 1988. College Station, Tex.: Texas Transportation Institute.

Hanson, R., ed. 1984. Perspectives on Urban infrastructure. Washington, D.C.: National Academy Press.

Henning, C., M. Lieberg, and K.P. Linden. 1991. Social Care and Local Networks, A Study of a Model for Public Social Services Applied in a New Suburban Area. Stockholm, Swedish Council for Building Research.

Herman, R., and J.H. Ausubel. 1988. Cities and Infrastructure: Synthesis and Perspectives. In Cities and Their Vital Systems, Infrastructure, Past, Present and Future, J.H. Ausubel and R. Herman, eds. Washington, D.C.: National Academy Press.

Khan, M. Shahbaz, 1987. Infrastructure and the Development Process. Background Paper for the World Development Report 1987. Washington, D.C.: World Bank

Kuhn, Thomas S. 1970. The Structure of Scientific Revolutions, 2nd edition. Chicago: University of Chicago Press.

Lee, K.S., J. Stein, and J. Lorentzen. 1986. Urban Infrastructure and Productivity: Issues for Investment and Operations and Maintenance, Washington, D.C: World Bank.

Marland, G., and A. Weinberg. 1988. Longevity of infrastructure. In Cities and their Vital Systems, J. Ausubel and R. Herman, eds. Washington, D.C.: National Academy Press.

Munnell, Alicia H. 1990. How does public infrastructure affect regional economic performance? In Is There a Shortfall in Public Capital Investment? Conference Series Number 34. Boston: Federal Reserve Bank of Boston.

NCPWI (National Council on Public Works Improvement). 1988. Fragile Foundations: A Report on America's Public Works. Washington, D.C.: U.S. Government Printing Office.

NIAC (National Infrastructure Advisory Committee). 1984. Hard Choices. Report to the Joint Economic Committee of the U.S. Congress. Washington, D.C.: Government Printing Office.

NRC (National Research Council). 1987. Infrastructure for the 21st Century. Committee on Infrastructure Innovation. Washington, D.C.: National Academy Press.

OTA (U.S. Congress, Office of Technology Assessment). 1991. Delivering the Goods: Public Works Technologies, Management, and Finance. OTA-SET-477. Washington, D.C.: U.S. Government Printing Office.

Peterson, G.E. 1979-1981. America's Urban Capital Stock (6 volumes). Washington, D.C.: The Urban Institute Press.

RERC (Real Estate Research Corporation). 1974. The Costs of Sprawl. Washington, D.C.: Council for Environmental Quality and Environmental Protection Agency.

Sanders, H.T. 1991. Public Works and Public Dollars: Federal Infrastructure Aid and Local Investment Policy. A Statement before the U.S. Congress, the House Wednesday Group (February 4, 1991), Washington, D.C.

Slovic, P., B. Fischoff, and S. Lichtenstein. 1985. Characterizing perceived risk. In Perilous Progress: Technology as Hazard. R.W. Kates, C. Hohenemser, and J. Kasperson, eds. Boulder, Co.: Westview Press.

White, D.C., C.J. Andrews, and N.W. Stauffer. 1992. The new team: Electricity sources without carbon dioxide. Technology Review (January):42-50.

World Bank. 1989. Sub-Saharan Africa: From Crisis to Sustainable Growth. Washington, D.C.

3

OBSERVING LOCALLY

Infrastructure is primarily local. Communities around the United States work to maintain, enhance, and develop the nation's infrastructure. The various infrastructure modes are organized and managed differently, but they come together in local areas as a system that supports the local economy and the community's well-being.

There have been notable successes in which local communities have been united and mobilized to come to grips with their infrastructure problems. The committee determined that identifying the common elements of these successes will give infrastructure planners, administrators, designers, builders, and operators better understanding and guidance in formulating development and management strategies. This guidance will in turn enhance—at the national level—the performance and efficiency of our aggregate investments in infrastructure.

THE COLLOQUIA SERIES

The committee undertook its colloquia as fact-finding workshops to explore success stories that illuminated cases of local progress in solving infrastructure problems. The term "success stories" was adopted for discussion, but it was agreed that unsuccessful (even disastrous) cases warrant consideration when transferable lessons can be learned.

The committee determined that several elements of these stories would be important to the study aims. First, successful (or not so successful) would be defined in the context of the specific community, as reported by local constituents.

Second, the cases examined should illustrate means for overcoming obstacles in the search for effective applications of infrastructure technology. While major enhancements or "quantum leaps" in infrastructure performance are of great interest, the committee also sought to document incremental improvements as

Box 3-1 Examples Considered for Case Study.

The committee considered a number of cases that might serve as the bases for colloquia, such as the following:

Boston, Mass. — major projects and interactions of government at several levels.

Cincinnati, Ohio — business-government coalition direct appeal to the local population to achieve consensus on repair needs and strategy.

Cleveland, Ohio — aftermath of fiscal crisis and aging systems.

Los Angeles, Calif. — air quality control as a force in transportation and municipal waste management.

New York City region — vulnerable systems, responses to system disruptions from major facility failures.

Phoenix, Ariz. — arts-engineering coalition in an area undergoing rapid growth.

Canadian National Railways — applications of acoustical monitoring for bridge condition assessment and maintenance management.

Mexico City, Mexico — environmental reclamation and restoration.

Nairobi, Kenya — private sector municipal waste management at low costs.

New Delhi, India — nongovernmental organizations mobilizing a range of environmentally more "friendly" infrastructure technologies.

Sao Paulo, Brazil — use of methane gas, from solid waste disposal, to operate transit vehicles.

Various areas — plastic and other polymeric linings for repair of concrete pipes and canals, and corrosion control on metal fittings in water supply and sewer subsystems.

well. The committee's aim in general would be to assess how the diffusion of beneficial new ideas into infrastructure practice occurs, and to identify ways to speed and enhance the effectiveness of this process.

Third, because infrastructures are typically so long-lived, the committee was particularly interested in cases of effective measurement, monitoring, and evaluation of life-cycle performance. Issues of standard setting and performance evaluation, and the balance between the benefits and costs of monitoring or assessment activities throughout the lifecycle, come into play in trying to determine the characteristics of a good infrastructure management system. Such a system would accommodate meaningful and practical consideration of the trade-offs among infrastructure's initial development (i.e., design and construction), operation, maintenance, and management costs, not only in planning and design but throughout the service life. Committee members were especially interested in data collection and management information systems, analytical models and other management tools to assist problem solving, system management tools well suited to the operation, maintenance, and asset management of existing systems rather than system expansion.

Fourth, and closely related to matters of life-cycle management, the committee sought to identify institutional structures that seem well suited to the management of infrastructure in the coming decades. Such structures might, for example, feature cooperative action (teaming) of private and public sectors at various levels, focus on users and their demand for and response to infrastructures, and emphasize specific and comprehensible desirable outcomes rather than abstract goals or objectives.

With these four broad aims in mind, the committee considered a wide range of international examples of "success stories." Examples were proposed initially on the basis of committee members' and staff knowledge of each situation (see Box 3-1). After some discussion, the committee developed a "short list" of examples for further consideration.

Foreign cases, drawn primarily from less developed countries, were quickly discarded as a basis for initial workshops. Useful information and transferable lessons are available from such examples, but the committee concluded that cultural, economic, and institutional differences would require more substantial data collection and analysis to develop convincing conclusions for application in the United States.

The committee then defined eight specific selection criteria as the basis for choosing locations that would accomplish the study's broad aims, by illustrating the following:

1. uses of innovative technology;
2. transferability of technology;
3. effectively overcoming barriers to the use of new technology;
4. constituency building and community support;
5. effective citizen involvement;
6. effective improvement of existing infrastructure (versus new building);
7. unique institutional approaches; and
8. effective application of life-cycle cost-benefit analysis as a management tool, particularly in the context of political decision-making.

After some additional data collection and discussion, the committee selected Phoenix, Cincinnati, and Boston as sites for the first three colloquia. Table 3-1 presents statistics characterizing the three areas.

A large number of people in each city participated in the committee's workshop and gave generously of their time and insights. Appendix C is a listing of these participants. Given more time and resources, the committee might have selected additional cities for study. The concerns of infrastructure in smaller communities and rural areas, for example, may differ from those in the medium and larger metropolitan areas included here. The experience of regions in which growth management strategies have been adopted (e.g., Miami, Florida; Portland, Oregon; communities in southern California) may differ from those in which economic losses have been more severe (e.g., Detroit, Michigan;

St. Louis, Missouri). Further variety in local government structure and metropolitan patterns of intergovernmental relationships warrants further attention as well. As a group, Phoenix, Cincinnati, and Boston represent a middle ground in size, complexity, and economic health. The range of experience may be widened in future studies.

In addition, some observers question whether these cases are indeed success stories. Phoenix, for example, is a sprawling metropolis that proponents of growth management cite as an example of why tighter land use, population growth, and environmental impact controls are needed. However, the city has consolidated its jurisdiction over the entire area and thereby eliminated many of the intergovernmental problems that older metropolitan areas face. Boston is dismissed by many observers as simply a case of "pork barrel" funding of transport and past failure to charge prices adequate to cover the real costs for water and sewer services. However, the region has survived decades of major economic change. In choosing these cases, the committee hoped to gain insight into the balance among such conflicting views of what is or should be happening in the nation's metropolitan areas.

PHOENIX, ARIZONA

The Committee on Infrastructure held its initial workshop colloquium in Phoenix, Arizona, on March 20 and 21, 1992. During the two days, the group visited several recently completed projects, observed broadly the elements of the city's infrastructure, and met with city and state government staff and members of community groups.

Background

Phoenix has been described by some residents as a city "at the threshold of maturity, evolving from a 'boomtown' into a cosmopolitan city." The city's desert setting, rapid growth, rich history,

Table 3-1 Summary Statistics on Workshop Cities

Statistics Category		Phoenix[a]	Cincinnati	Boston
Year of settlement		1864	1789	1630
Current population	City[b]	983,403	364,040	574,283
	PMSA[c]	2,122,000*	1,453,000	2,871,000
	CMSA[c]	NA	1,744,000	4,172,000
Current land area	City[d]	419.9 square mile	77.2 square mile	48.4 square mile
Per capita income	CMSA[e]	18,042*	18,632	24,315
Minority populations	City[f]	Black: 5.2% Hispanic: 20.0%	Black: 37.9% Hispanic: 0.7%	Black: 25.6% Hispanic: 10.8%
	CMSA[g]	Black: 3.5% Hispanic: 16.3%*	Black: 11.7% Hispanic: 0.5%	Black: 5.7% Hispanic: 4.6%
Labor force	PMSA[h]	Total employed: 1,028,100	Total employed: 754,100	Total employed: 1,481,600
		Unemployment: 4.3%[a]	Unemployment: 4.2%	Unemployment: 5.1%
Cost of living index	PMSA[i]	101.7*	105.8	134.8
One-parent households	CMSA[j]	73,000*	64,000	118,000

42

Notes:

CMSA = consolidated metropolitan statistical area (Cincinnati CMSA, which lies in Ohio, Kentucky, and Indiana; includes the Hamilton, Kentucky area; Boston CMSA, which lies in Mass. and New Hampshire, includes the Lawrence and Salem, Mass., metropolitan areas);

MSA = metropolitan statistical area;

NA = not available;

NECMA = New England County metropolitan area;

PMSA = primary metropolitan statistical area (Cincinnati PMSA includes areas in Kentucky and Indiana);

"The revised definitions [of different MSA's] appear in OMB [Office of Management and Budget] press release 83-20 of June 27, 1983. The official standards for defining MSA's appeared in the Federal Register, January 3, 1980 (part 6)" (Bureau of the Census, 1992, p. 896).

[a] For Phoenix, all metropolitan area data is for its MSA, which includes all of Maricopa County.

[b] The World Almanac and Book of Facts (1992, pp. 132-133)

[c] Bureau of the Census (1992, pp. 898-904).

[d] Bureau of the Census (1992, pp. 35-37).

[e] Bureau of the Census (1992, p. 440). Information is taken from April 1992 Survey of Current Business, Bureau of Economic Analysis, U.S. Department of Commerce. The numbers are for 1990. For Boston, the designated area is its NECMA (Boston-Lawrence-Salem-Lowell-Brockton, Mass.).

[f] Bureau of the Census (1992, p. 35).

[g] Bureau of the Census (1992, p. 34).

[h] Bureau of the Census (1992, p. 385). Labor force is defined as "the civilian noninstitutional population 16 years old and over."

[i] Bureau of the Census (1992, pp. 474-475). Measures "relative price levels for consumer goods and services in particular areas for midmanagement standard of living." National average = 100.

[j] Bureau of the Census (1992, p. 50).

43

and cultural diversity have been important factors shaping this transition, making Phoenix and Arizona as a whole into what some people have termed "the new California, a place where palm trees and the desert still beckon dreamers" (Johnson, 1991). Very rapid growth in recent years is measured by a more than 30 percent increase in Phoenix's population during the 1980s and even greater rates in surrounding communities. Phoenix is now the tenth largest city in the United States.

With very low-density urbanization, the incorporated area of Phoenix and surrounding communities is approximately 1,000 square miles, several times the size of other urban regions with similar populations. Some 50 percent of the land remains undeveloped. Phoenix encompasses large areas of open space reserve, notably in the mountain preserves, and South Mountain Park is, at 17,000 acres, the nation's largest city park.

The Salt River Valley, in which Phoenix is located, bears the mark of more than 1,000 years of infrastructure development. The modern settlement of Phoenix began in the late 1860s with construction of irrigation works built on the remains of ancient canals. Archaeologists have traced an extensive system developed by the Hohokam Indians that encompassed more than 300 miles of major canals and 950 miles of lesser canals by approximately A.D. 1450, all constructed with wood and stone tools and manual labor. The disappearance of these canal builders (named Ho Ho Kam— those who have gone—by subsequent native tribes) is attributed by some to extended drought and by others to flood-caused damage and subsequent failure of the canal system. The mythical Phoenix, rising from the ashes of this early civilization, was adopted by early white settlers as a symbol for the community.

The modern city and the state of Arizona are the sites of major, noteworthy, and sometimes controversial infrastructure investments such as the Central Arizona Project (water supply), Phoenix Sky Harbor Airport, and highway Interstate 10. Such projects have often reflected a major national resolve, made in earlier decades, to settle the nation's West and a consequent willingness to invest national resources out of proportion to the region's population and development at the time of decision.

However, as in other areas, these major investments have not always been viewed with favor by the residents of areas where construction is planned. Famed architect Frank Lloyd Wright, for example, fought against installation of electric power transmission lines that would bring energy to the growing city but would also, in his view, spoil the desert vista from his winter studio and home.

An important element in the completion of a number of the city's most recent infrastructure projects has been a unique coalition of the arts and public works communities that has fostered imaginative ways of dealing with community concerns and enhanced the levels of communication and trust between infrastructure professionals and the public at large.

How did this coalition develop, and how important has it been to success in infrastructure development? Has Phoenix been unusually successful in its ability to achieve high infrastructure performance through effective management and adoption of state-of-the-art technology? These are some of the questions the committee considered during its visit to Phoenix.

The committee was hosted and guided by the directors of the Public Works Department and the Phoenix Arts Commission, members of their staffs, consultants to their agencies, and staff of other city and state agencies. For a portion of both days, the committee visited infrastructure and urban development sites in Phoenix. Each site visited offered unique perspectives on the relationship between infrastructure technology and the community.

Asphalt Pavement Using Recycled Rubber Tires and Other Design Features

The committee observed that Phoenix makes extensive use of asphalt concrete for paving and overlays of city streets. Extreme summer temperatures, routinely exceeding 100°F, pose particular problems for pavement design and construction in the region.

Some years ago, an engineer for the city of Phoenix developed the idea that ground rubber from waste vehicular tires might be used as an asphalt additive to improve overlay adhesion and hot-weather performance. Experiments and subsequent applications of the idea demonstrated that the new mix not only had superior working characteristics and physical behavior, but resisted bleaching in the Arizona sun and resulted in a 10-decibel reduction in tirepavement noise, compared to conventional pavements. The city now uses rubber from approximately 300,000 recycled tires annually, and suppliers are preparing to market recycled rubber to other regions.[9]

The city permitted the engineer to patent the rubber additive technology, subject to granting Phoenix the right to use it without paying royalties. The engineer profited from the patent, and the city has saved substantial amounts compared to royalties that would have been paid had the technology been developed and patented elsewhere. The committee felt that this case illustrates well a major incentive for any unit of government to encourage innovation among staff.[10]

In planning for the future, certain Phoenix streets and highways have been designed with centerline right-of-way space designated for the development of rail or restricted-guideway bus transit systems. On city arterials, this area is given special surface treatment or lane marking. The committee also visited the Central Avenue Beautification Project and Dunlop Avenue in Sunnyslope, areas in which community groups have worked with the Phoenix

---

[9]The Strategic Highway Research Program reports that about 250 million automobile tires and 25 million truck tires are disposed of annually. These wastes are nearly indestructible and pose fire, health, and other safety and environmental problems at sites around the country. However, tests to date suggest that the performance of rubber and asphalt pavements varies substantially with climatic conditions and construction problems can arise. The technology thus may not work equally well in all regions and remains controversial.

[10]Disincentives and obstacles to innovation are the subject of another BRB report, *The Role of Public Agencies in Fostering New Technology and Innovation in Building* (Dibner and Lemer, 1992).

Arts Commission to achieve neighborhood improvement through sidewalk reconstruction, street landscaping, and placement of art inspired by local history or artifacts of prehistoric Indian cultures.

Papago Freeway and Margaret Hance Park

More than 20 years in the planning, the recently completed Papago Freeway is the final link in the Interstate 10 coast-to-coast highway, a subject of long-term controversy and a construction project characterized by its designers as "among America's most unique urban highway ventures." Complex design features and extensive landscaping, customized noise barriers, and other measures were employed to mitigate adverse environmental impact on the communities adjacent to the highway. Extended below-grade construction, combined with two major multiroad elevated interchanges (termed locally the "Stack" and "Short Stack"), made this highway particularly costly to construct. Slightly more than 94 percent of the construction costs were paid by federal program funds.

One major element of both mitigation and cost is the 29-acre Margaret Hance Park, of which 13 acres have been newly constructed atop a half-mile-long tunnel through which the freeway passes. This park, located at the intersection with Central Avenue, one of Phoenix's major arterials, is meant to serve nearby residents and office workers, bus riders using the transit station (provisions for future higher-volume modes have been made here also), and Phoenix residents and tourists expected to visit the attractions or special outdoor events planned for the park. City staff acknowledged that drainage maintenance problems have been encountered and explained the special design provisions to address safety concerns posed by possible vehicle accidents in the enclosed roadway below the park. The park itself served as an amenity that enabled the freeway's completion, balancing community concerns in the political forum in which decisions were made.

A prominent feature of the Papago Freeway, found also in other Phoenix highways, is a design profile intended to assist with flood control in adjacent neighborhoods. For example, noise barriers are equipped with holes at street level to permit storm-water to flow onto the highway when the capacity of neighborhood street drainage facilities is exceeded by peak runoff volumes.

Squaw Peak Parkway and Thomas Road Overpass

Touring the Squaw Peak Parkway and adjacent neighborhoods, the committee had an opportunity to observe products of Phoenix's use of art to enhance visual and cultural aspects of the urban environment and to mitigate adverse impact of infrastructure. Jointly financed by the city of Phoenix and the Arizona Department of Transportation, the highway itself reflects a relatively unusual balancing of typically conflicting planning and design objectives: the widths of right-of-way and roadway lanes were narrowed to reduce land taking and neighborhood disruption, while maintaining highway safety; pedestrian, bicycle, and equestrian amenities are included; pedestrian bridges were treated as urban design elements rather than simply utilitarian constructions.

The Thomas Road Overpass is claimed by many to be the outstanding success of the Squaw Peak Parkway. By drawing on the "one percent for art" funds earmarked by the city's voters in a $1 billion capital improvement bond issue in 1988, an artist was made part of the design team from the early stages of design. The artist asked key questions of the structural designers regarding the rationale for the standard span length used on other highway overpass bridges. The questioning, motivated by the artist's own concerns for the work to be installed subsequently on the overpass, led the structural designers to rethink their assumptions and develop a custom bridge design. The changes were estimated to have saved about $1 million in construction costs, an amount more than four times the artist's fees and expenses to execute the art work.

The artist's work, primarily in adobe applied with the help of residents drawn from the neighborhood and citywide, includes frog-shaped structural columns inspired by Hohokam artifacts and

Figure 3-A

By questioning the state's standard bridge design originally planned for the Thomas Road Overpass, part of the Squaw Peak Parkway in Phoenix, the artist invited to "beautify" an austere structure motivated a money-saving custom design and created an award-winning community asset.

murals incorporating neighborhood artifacts as well as traditional symbols. The engineers who participated in the design describe the bridge, according to local newspaper reports, as "a structure like no other."

Phoenix's Percent for Art Program, administered by the Phoenix Art Commission according to city documents, was established to acquire works of art that "enhance the aesthetic quality of public spaces and advance public understanding of art." One percent of the city's annual capital construction budget is set aside for the program. Placing artists on the public works design team is only one element of the program. A Project Art Plan, developed and maintained by the Arts Commission with help from community members, artists, and staff of city departments, includes integration of artworks into construction projects, purchasing or commissioning artworks after construction, and interactive projects for artists to work with community groups to produce artworks.

In contrast to the generally acclaimed Thomas Road overpass, the installations of artworks along the Squaw Peak Parkway south of Glendale Avenue have been more controversial. Some 35 sculptures were commissioned to adorn noise barriers and adjoining landscaped areas in an effort to mitigate the intrusion of the highway cutting through older neighborhoods whose residents had unsuccessfully fought construction. Out-of-state designers selected by the Arts Commission produced brightly colored concrete and ceramic vases and teapots, intended—according to commission staff—to create a bridge of everyday objects between residents and the highway. Underlying the design approach was an effort to rethink the nature of the wall produced by the highway and its noise barriers. Press reports of residents' initial response varied from "unfavorable" to "outraged," and the city's entire public art program seemed threatened.

However, neighborhood anger may have been generated by disruptions associated with the taking of land and construction of the highway itself, and the art works provided an immediate focus. In June 1992, just four months after the controversy, the artwork and landscape project along the Squaw Peak Parkway won a prestigious local design award as the year's best public art project.

By the fall of 1992, reports in local and national publications suggested that the community was taking delight in this new landmark linear work of art.

27th Avenue Solid Waste Management Facility

Another application of the Percent for Art Program is Phoenix's 27th Avenue Solid Waste Management Facility, still under construction when the committee visited. This multifunctional facility will accommodate solid waste transfer from collection truck to large trailer haulers, materials sorting for recycling, mulching of yard and wood wastes, and educational programs targeted at school children and tourists. Public works personnel envision the facility as a future attraction comparable to the sewers of Paris in the nineteenth century or to major U.S. airports in the early years of commercial aviation.

There are many similarities with the Thomas Road Overpass. The Arts Commission and Public Works Department worked together, adding artists to the design team. The artists spurred the designers to change, and construction bids some $2 million below estimates quieted skeptics concerned that the artists' involvement would increase costs.

Seeking to design a facility that would illustrate principles of structural design as well as waste management for children and adults, the team developed a structural system that placed the primary structural element outside the building. Large steel trusses above the roof will be clearly visible as visitors approach the facility, and riveted joints, although infrequent in current construction, enhance the aesthetic appeal of the structure under closer scrutiny. Determined to attract public participation in the city's planned recycling program, the team designed catwalks, an amphitheater, and other elements to permit visitors to observe and learn how the municipal wastes are processed, how the facility works, and the more basic problems of waste management and environmental protection. A planned pond system adjacent to the facility and the nearby Salt River will demonstrate the use of natural processes for sewage treatment and extend an existing wetlands area that serves as a small bird sanctuary.

The facility's location at the existing (but soon to be closed) landfill site not only overcame community resistance to new construction, but actually attracted vocal community support for the facility. Tipping fees at this and other city landfills were raised from unrealistically low levels (enabled for decades by the use of abandoned gravel pits along the river), ensuring the financial feasibility of recycling and the transfer operation.

Water Resources and Canals

Located in a hot desert environment, Phoenix demonstrates very effectively the truth of an early observation that "where water flows, life grows." Visitors to Phoenix neighborhoods cannot fail to be impressed by the differences in landscaping between areas served by government-provided irrigation and those without such service. In the areas served, residents flood-irrigate their properties with untreated water on a once or twice weekly basis. Generally open canals run parallel to streets and sidewalks. Landscaping in neighborhoods lacking access to canal irrigation typically depends on native desert plant materials and exposed soil and rock (i.e., xeroscaping).

The Salt River Project (SRP), a water and power utility that supplies approximately half of the Phoenix area's water and one-half to two-thirds of its electricity, is the oldest multipurpose project authorized under the Federal Reclamation Act of 1902. The price for water, uniform regardless of use, is heavily subsidized by power sales, and users are charged approximately one-sixth of the estimated production cost (per acre-foot).

The major canals, those of both the SRP and other projects, are gaining increasing recognition and use as public amenities and urban design elements. The Arizona State University's recently completed Metropolitan Canal Study, funded by the National Endowment for the Arts, the Salt River Project, and the seven Valley Cities of the Phoenix Region, with support by the Junior

Figure 3-B

The engineer-artist team responsible for design of Phoenix's 27th Avenue Solid Waste Management Facility, here under construction, created an entry to the building that would illustrate to the public something about how structures work.

League of Phoenix, explored multiple use of canals as "places for people." The Phoenix area is very widely spread, development densities are quite low, and approximately 50 percent of the land in Phoenix is undeveloped. The canals represent a possible means for directing development into efficient forms. SRP rights of way are used for siting power transmission lines, and the city is developing canal demonstration plans, a multidepartment and citizen effort to demonstrate ways to maximize the recreational and scenic value of some 78 miles of Salt River Project and other canals in Phoenix. Plans involve improved access between the canals and adjacent commercial properties, reorientation of development, and community education. Funding for the activity is provided by special budget allocations, eliminating any possible competition between these plans and other municipal needs.

A major canal maintenance problem is the growth of moss in the canals, which consumes water and—left unchecked—can block flow entirely. The SRP is exploring the use of new machinery that can operate from the bank or in the canal. Use is also being made of a specially bred fish, the white amur, a type of grass carp originally found in China, which consumes large quantities of vegetation (and reportedly jumps from the water to reach vegetation along the banks). The fish are sterilized, and grates are installed at canal gates to prevent their breeding and entering natural waterways.

The occasional but very heavy desert rainstorms with high peak flows of stormwater runoff have led not only to special highway design features already noted, but also to major diversion facilities. All extensive developments must provide retention basins on-site, and Phoenix has numerous areas that combine stormwater retention basins and drainage swales with parks and open space. These projects (one visited was "Desert Storm" Park) serve as community recreational facilities and amenities most of the time, but also provide important flood protection and runoff management services.

Serving on a much larger scale is the Arizona Canal Diversion Channel (ACDC), designed and constructed by the Army Corps of Engineers (using federal funds) with sponsorship of the Flood

Control District of Maricopa County. The channel protects developed areas by intercepting floodwaters and urban runoff. The ACDC follows the Arizona Canal and is intended to eliminate overtopping and levee failures caused by major storms. The design is based on the estimated 100-year storm. A variety of problems arising in design and construction, due to failure to work with the community, have been addressed by enhancing the visual design of channel fencing, provision of pedestrian facilities, and other amenities.

Grass-Roots Initiative and Sunnyslope Village

The Phoenix's Sunnyslope area, northwest of downtown Phoenix and at the foot of one of the city's mountain reserves, has evolved since its original development several decades ago into a diverse set of communities. One of these communities, faced with the threat of urban redevelopment planned from outside, undertook a grass-roots initiative to preserve the area and enhance its infrastructure. The Sunnyslope Village Alliance has been an active force in bringing together the community, government staff, and outside advisers, to ensure that the community's priorities are reflected in how urban development resources are used. The alliance's Community Planning and Design Committee has undertaken its own planning and design initiatives while working actively with city agencies to ensure that neighborhood concerns are understood and considered.

Concern about the conflict between narrow sidewalks and fast-moving traffic along Dunlop Avenue led to early action to improve safety and amenity by widening the sidewalks and installing landscaping and artist-designed tree guards. The Percent for Art Program was utilized, with community residents participating in all aspects of this project.

The Sunnyslope Transit Center, a bus route terminus, also bears the mark of the Percent for Art Program, in the form of sculptures produced by a collaboration of a professional artist and local school children. In addition, the center includes a technically innovative bus shelter designed with a "cooling tower" that offers waiting passengers relief of about 20-30 degrees from ambient hot summer temperatures. Such shelters are relatively low cost, approximately $30,000 currently, and are expected to decline in cost as the numbers produced increase. When a prototype unit on loan to the city was about to be removed at the end of a summer's free trial period, the bus-riding community was instrumental in convincing city officials of the value of these shelters.

How Representative Is the Phoenix Experience?

There are questions, of course, whether the experience of Phoenix projects is replicable in other communities. High percentages of federal funding, rapid economic growth, low land prices, low density and availability of undeveloped land, and a governmental structure relatively congenial to innovation are among the factors that distinguish Phoenix from many other communities and may limit the ability of other communities to emulate its experience.

The degree of recognition of the importance of maintenance and longer-term commitment to the full costs of ownership is difficult to observe in a community undergoing very rapid growth. Most federal programs that finance or otherwise influence infrastructure emphasize new construction and fail to confront maintenance issues. A significant conflict with efficiency and reliability is introduced by the typical reluctance, on the part of elected officials and the public, to consider the full costs of ownership when making major investment decisions. The major federal input to highway and water projects in Phoenix suggests that federal programs favoring new construction of large projects may introduce significant distortions in the efficient and equitable distribution of investment and management efforts among regions and in development patterns within regions.

The institutional structure of Phoenix's public works seems to have made infrastructure innovation somewhat easier than in many other cities. Although there is the usual patchwork of agencies operating in the region, the Phoenix city government system—a strong city manager form, with strict separation of the city council from executive agencies—encourages enthusiastic and committed professionalism among city staff and facilitates the taking of calculated risks.

However, this ability to take calculated risks clearly has limits. The public has a limited appreciation of the value of public works investment and innovation and of the inherent uncertainties in trying new things. Government officials, both elected and professional staff, are themselves at risk, and when public controversy erupts even because of external events (e.g., changes in fiscal condition or political balance), the positive assessments that motivated decisions may be forgotten or reversed.

In addition, innovations on some projects may reflect simply changes in general practice or the availability of new products that enable activities that were previously too difficult, costly, or simply impossible. Current projects (like the Papago Freeway and Squaw Peak Parkway) are frequently the result of decades of discussion and planning, and so can take advantage of new technology (e.g., improved pavement materials, electronic traffic control devices, enhanced vehicle safety) to enhance the benefits and reduce the adverse impact of infrastructures.

Nevertheless, the Phoenix experience demonstrates how important continuing community involvement in infrastructure planning and development can be to successful project development. The use of public art and the coalition between the arts and public works communities provide a metaphor for this involvement, both successfully and not so successfully accomplished. The importance of community involvement extends well beyond simply easing the introduction of infrastructure into the community. In the context of multiple agencies pursuing their specific missions, the local public forum may be the most effective—and possibly the only feasible—mechanism for resolving conflicting objectives and counterproductive actions. To encourage involvement, many infrastructure projects in Phoenix have seemingly been given a relatively long time for planning.

On the other hand, the local forum cannot deal effectively with issues of the interregional allocation of infrastructure resources. The national political forum wherein needs are determined and investment priorities established seemingly deals poorly with intersectoral linkages (i.e., among water, transport, waste, and other infrastructure subsystems).

Extracting More General Principles

Some aspects of the Phoenix experience seem clearly to be replicable (i.e., to offer lessons for other cities and national policy):

• If infrastructure is viewed as a flow of services, then those responsible for providing infrastructure should seek to ensure that the supply of these services is reliable and efficient. The Salt River Project and Phoenix Public Works Department include reliability among their goals, and an entrepreneurial approach to their affairs has helped ensure efficiency.

• Bringing new points of view into the infrastructure management team, as the cases of the Thomas Road overpass and the 27th Avenue Solid Waste Management Facility illustrate, can be a very productive means for achieving innovation. New ideas were introduced that saved money and improved performance. Creative management by the Arts Commission and the Public Works Department have made the Percent for Art Program a highly effective mechanism for broadening the membership of the infrastructure team. Similarly, the Sunnyslope Village Alliance learned that some technological improvements may obscure the real issues or impacts of infrastructure, such as when infrastructure professionals depend uncritically on the results produced by analytical models (e.g., forecasting future traffic or rainfall). Permitting (and encouraging) new segments of the community (e.g., artists, neighborhood groups) to participate actively in the provision of infrastructure helps to ensure that questions are raised about the technologies employed, questions that can lead to rethinking of assumptions.

- Working to achieve multifunctional use of infrastructure sites (e.g., parks over highways, streets and transitways, solid waste and sewage treatment) may be an important policy for maximizing efficiency in land use, controlling risk, and reducing community resistance to infrastructure. Because conflicting objectives and counterproductive actions will inevitably occur in the development and management of urban infrastructure, projects that serve more than one end or solve more than one problem are more likely to be successful.

- Infrastructure design has important implications for what urban designers may term "quality of place," the characteristics (or ambience) that are a significant element of a community's quality of life and the acceptance of the infrastructure project. Concern for the aesthetics of infrastructure does not necessarily increase costs and may be viewed better as an essential rather than a luxury.

- Infrastructure facilities can play a useful educational role as an instrument for teaching children and adults about stewardship of the natural and built environment, science, and mathematics. Infrastructure professionals (e.g., urban designers, municipal engineers, landscape architects, planners, public administrators) can be educated as well, to enhance their sensitivity to community concerns and the opportunities for innovation. Such education should always continue "on the job," but there may be improvements that university professional training programs could make to foster appreciation of the teamwork required to achieve effective infrastructure.

- There are benefits to be gained by both the individuals who develop a new idea and the city or other government agency that fosters the individual creativity in introducing infrastructure innovation. The Phoenix experience typifies the win-win character of principles and strategies for infrastructure improvement, for which the committee was searching.

CINCINNATI, OHIO

The Committee on Infrastructure held its second workshop colloquium in Cincinnati, Ohio, on June 5 and 6, 1992. During the two days, the group met with city government staff and elected officials, business leaders, and members of community groups; visited several ongoing and recently completed projects; and observed other elements of the city's infrastructure.

Background

Cincinnati, Queen City on the Ohio River, was founded shortly after the American Revolution and by the middle of the nineteenth century was a booming frontier river town. Tourist brochures quote Charles Dickens, who journeyed down the Ohio River by steamboat in 1842, as finding it "a beautiful city; cheerful, thriving and animated." For the two decades before the Civil War, Cincinnati was the fastest growing city west of the Alleghenies and the sixth largest in the United States. Although the war brought a sharp decline in river trade and Chicago became the nation's inland commercial capital, Cincinnati's past left both the city and the region a rich legacy of industry and business participation in the community, as well as a pattern of urban development that frames its present situation.

Built on steep hills and bluffs overlooking the Ohio River and tributaries, present-day Cincinnati has some 25 miles of municipally owned retaining walls—more than any other city in the United States. A relatively compact downtown area that is largely separated from the river by highways and sports facilities features the "nation's most complete skyway system." Much of this system, which remains open to public use 24 hours per day, is maintained by city crews under contract to more than 30 property owners through whose buildings the walkways pass.

The city of Cincinnati lies within the boundaries of Hamilton County, where there are 49 local governments and county commissions that share responsibilities for government. The nine members of the Cincinnati City Council are all elected at-large, and the member receiving the largest number of votes in the biennial election is named mayor. A professional city manager is responsible for administration of the city's activities. Cincinnati was among the first cities in the nation to adopt a manager-council form of government.

A network of 51 distinct and officially recognized community subareas in the city provides a channel for community activists to represent neighborhood interests. Each of these recognized community councils receives $10,000 in funding annually from the city (subject to certain qualifying conditions and requirements), to support communication and volunteer activities under the Neighborhood Support Program (NSP).

Several decades of declining population and tax base, aging facilities[11], and expansion of city boundaries driven, in part by the lucrative profitability of the city's water supply utility,[12] resulted in what some have termed a "classic big city infrastructure crisis." Alarmed by the level and rate of physical deterioration, city staff began to document that crisis in *The Public Works Story*, an annual report prepared by the Department of Public Works and published in the years 1983 through 1988. The report was widely circulated, contributing to public awareness and understanding of the need for improvements.

This report set the stage for a series of institutional changes, remarkable by comparison with many other cities facing similar

---

[11]City staff estimated 90 percent of Cincinnati's infrastructure to be more than 50 years old, and at least 30 percent to be more than 100 years old.

[12]Until 1948, suburban areas could obtain city water, but only under a binding agreement that the area served would be annexed to the city when it became contiguous to the city. The utility's profitability, without consideration of other municipal costs, made expansion of its service seem advantageous, and city boundaries grew. However, a change in state law prohibited the annexation requirement, and a city earnings tax was ultimately instituted.

problems, that comprised the focus of the committee's visit to Cincinnati.

The Stormwater Management Utility

Even before *The Public Works Story* began to appear, stormwater management was a public concern. Some 25 years of urban growth combined with inadequate budgets for both maintenance and new development of drainage facilities had given rise to serious flooding in several areas of Cincinnati. By the mid-1980s there were some 10,000 unresolved complaints from property owners regarding blocked, inadequate, and needed drains and sewers.

Much of the city is served by a combined system that handles stormwater runoff and sanitary and industrial wastewater. Begun in 1828 as a storm system only, the sewers were converted to serve both purposes late in the nineteenth century and expanded with that dual purpose until the early 1940s. Since then, most expansion has been undertaken with the separation of stormwater and sanitary flows. About 85 percent (in terms of miles of sewer line) is in the combined system. Hamilton County owns and the city operates this system, which passes about 25 percent of Cincinnati's annual sanitary sewage load untreated into the Ohio River in the course of some 70 storm overflow events.

Staff of Cincinnati's Department of Public Works (DPW) began in the early 1980s to conduct background studies and search for new ways to finance the stormwater management system. An early analysis was a simple mapping of the locations of citizen complaints about runoff and drainage. This map demonstrated graphically that the problems were citywide, and helped the DPW to gain the city council's understanding and support of the need to take action.

Drawing on experience from other parts of the United States, city staff proposed that a utility user service fee might be established to support stormwater system improvement. In addition, DPW staff recognized that a central point of management responsibility was needed. After more than two years of studies and public meetings, the Cincinnati City Council in 1984 (acting under a provision of the Ohio constitution) established the Stormwater Management Utility (SMU), administered as a division of the DPW.

The SMU's purpose is to provide for effective management and financing of a public stormwater system within the city. That system now includes some 250 miles of storm sewers (accounting for about 15 percent of Cincinnati's sewer system). The utility was given responsibility for inspection, construction, operation, and maintenance of city-owned drainage facilities under the control of the DPW, and provision was made for a system of "reasonable" service charges to finance SMU activities. The utility was also given regulatory responsibilities for ensuring public safety with regard to privately owned facilities.

Initial activities of the SMU were concentrated on making improvements that the public could readily observe, using a "worst-first" approach to setting priorities. These activities included cleaning drains that had long been clogged, responding quickly to calls during storms, and repairing notoriously deficient drainage structures. However, awareness of the SMU increased more rapidly than the utility's ability to make improvements, and there was an initially high incidence of complaints that taxed SMU's telephone system. The fact that the system was able to remain responsive was probably crucial to the utility's acceptance. Currently the utility maintains a target of response to all complaints within 72 hours.

There was initially no comprehensive data base to support assessment and collection of the user charge. The property tax rolls, which provided the starting point, excluded tax-exempt properties. A telephone response system was established to answer property owners' questions and register complaints, and special efforts were made in the early weeks of the new program to ensure responsiveness.

An effort was made to ensure that the billing system remained simple. Property owners pay a charge based on property type: one-to-two family residential, less than 10,000 square feet, $15.36 per year; one to two family residential, greater than 10,000 square feet, $21.50 per year; for all others, rates are based on site development intensity and coverage. After some five years of experience, the utility found that not everyone was receiving a bill. A task force was established to find ways to correct that situation. Current experience is that there is approximately 90 percent compliance and payment, without significant enforcement effort. About one-third of the utility's revenue, currently some $4.5 million annually, is derived from residential properties. The overall investment cost of implementing the stormwater plan was estimated to be approximately $120 million.

The utility has developed a total Stormwater Wastewater Integrated Management master plan that looks 50 to 100 years to the future to identify needs and current priorities for dealing with local surface drainage problems and unimproved streets. The planners have sought to address issues at a drainage basin level, but there has as yet been no substantial effort to take advantage of the underlying natural hydrological patterns in planning Cincinnati's stormwater drainage.

In addition, some areas continue to have complaints. Residents of the Hartwell community, for example, cite the city's failure to construct sewers and improve streets promised under the 1912 agreement that incorporated the area into Cincinnati. The low-lying area experiences flooding that has been exacerbated by the construction of new highway, as well as road improvements and related clearing of vegetation in neighboring communities. The SMU has attempted to construct dry wells to reduce the flooding problems, but poor maintenance and the depth of the water table have made them less successful than anticipated. The SMU estimates that dealing effectively with Hartwell's problems could cost some $7 million, a significant amount in terms of the utility's total budget, and would involve construction of retention caverns in the limestone beneath the community, a proposal that is outside the scope of SMU authority and, in addition, has elicited vocal community resistance.

The Infrastructure Commission

In a sense, establishment of the SMU foreshadowed formation of Cincinnati's Infrastructure Commission, a highly effective strategy that culminated in passage of a new tax referendum and initiation of the city's major Infrastructure Improvement Program. The commission and the consequent program were interesting models of how a community can mobilize resources to manage its infrastructure.

In 1986, in response to growing recognition that the city's infrastructure needed attention, city council asked John Smale—at that time Chief Executive Officer of Procter & Gamble, Cincinnati's largest employer—to serve as chairman of an independent commission to assess the situation and make recommendations for bringing the city's physical assets back to good condition and appearance. The council and the city's administration offered the commission the full cooperation of all city government departments in the commission's work.

In setting up this commission, the city was building on previous experience with commissions. Earlier in the decade, a group of business leaders had come together to study the operation of the city administration. This group, popularly called the "Phillips committee" (in recognition of its chairman), recommended changes in city administration to enhance efficiency and save taxpayer money, but concluded also that the professionalism and performance of the city's civil service staff were indeed quite high. The committee's work and recommendations gained council approval (about three-quarters were adopted, according to editorial comments in one of Cincinnati's leading newspapers) and convinced the business community that it could work productively with the city. The stage was thus set for effective cooperation between the city and the business community in addressing its infrastructure problems.

As the commission's chairman, Mr. Smale called on 10 other community leaders, primarily from the business community, to serve with him. These leaders, in turn, recruited other participants from throughout the business community. In the commission's report to the city council, presented on December 3, 1987,

Figure 3-C

Accumulated "superficial" deterioration and subsequent structural damage on Cincinnati's Ludlow Viaduct were a direct result of the neglect of maintenance, attributable to legislative budgetary decisions. Until repairs could be made, the bridge had to be closed to truck traffic, adding substantially to street congestion and the costs to businesses located in the area.

Mr. Smale cited the work of almost 200 volunteers who had contributed more than 10,000 person-hours over the course of the previous year to accomplishing the commission's charge. The commission—and Mr. Smale, in particular—participated in extensive public meetings in Cincinnati's local areas to enhance public understanding and support of the commission's work and recommendations. Publishers of the city's two principal newspapers and other media representatives were involved in the commission's work, resulting in thorough news coverage of the report.

The business community took on the responsibility for ensuring passage of the tax increase (described below) recommended by the commission to finance infrastructure, donating some $125,000 to prepare and circulate a videotaped presentation, a television commercial, and ads in local papers and to recruit volunteers to provide information to voters at the polls. The 1988 referendum was accepted by voters, although by a very narrow margin of fewer than 300 votes out of some 50,000 ballots cast.

Prominently featured in the materials prepared to present the commission's work and recommendations to the community were the ideas that infrastructure represents the city's physical assets— which the commission estimated to have a replacement value of $10.2 billion—and that these assets, properly used, make the area more competitive in attracting business and tourism. In his letter transmitting the commission's report to the mayor and council members, Mr. Smale also cited the goal that the plan would restore Cincinnati's infrastructure as a "source of pride and enjoyment to the people of this region," for today and succeeding generations.

The Smale commission drew heavily on information provided by city staff and technical resources within the private sector to conduct its assessment and develop recommendations. The commission's report included 100 specific recommendations covering planning, repairs, new construction, and financing. Cost estimates for these actions dealt explicitly with both a "one-time catch-up" amount of $217.3 million needed to correct the effect of past neglect and the $29.8 million in increased yearly spending needed for ongoing operations and maintenance. In selecting this package, the commission's infrastructure improvement program neglected some elements of infrastructure that, although warranting attention, were judged to fit less well into a feasible program (e.g., cyclical replacement of fire hydrants, maintenance and upgrading of telecommunications for police and fire services, additional data collection, and study of sewer and slope stability problems).

The commission devoted considerable attention to the potential sources of funding for these improvements. Approximately half of the funds were to come from enterprise funds, accounts deriving income from user charges and other fees for city garages, water supply, rubbish collection, and stormwater management. One unusual but important revenue source was the city's Cincinnati-to-Chattanooga rail line. This line, acquired in the nineteenth Century, is leased to Southern Railway. Renegotiation of the lease terms, initiated prior to the Smale commission's work, and a threatened court action against the railroad yielded a substantial one-time payment and increased annual revenues that are available for servicing and repayment of bonded debt.

The balance of funding was recommended to come from the city's general fund, and a package of new or enhanced revenue sources was specified. Recognition of the problems that had led to neglect of maintenance in the past, the centerpiece of the commission's recommendations was a dedicated general fund revenue increase, generated primarily from a small rate increase in the city's earnings tax (paid by employees working in Cincinnati and collected as a payroll deduction), from 2 to 2.1 percent, that would have to be spent on infrastructure. Rate increases or new taxes were recommended for gasoline, auto registration, sidewalk maintenance, tree planing and maintenance, and other city services as well.

The legislation developed to implement the earnings tax increase included the provision that failure of the city to appropriate and spend funds at the recommended levels would result in reversion of the tax rate to its initial 2 percent level. A formula and index were defined as the basis for determining the amount to be spent in future years, referenced to growth in the Commerce Department's implicit price deflator (based initially on gross national product but changed by the department in 1992, to gross domestic product or growth in the city's general fund revenues, whichever is less.[13] City staff found the crafting of this amendment to the income tax chapter of the Cincinnati Municipal Code to be a complex task. Realistic allowance had to be made for the time required to increase spending levels without gross inefficiencies and for the inability of current officials to impose on future officials an absolute requirement for spending. Annual certification that the appropriation and spending have met requirements is necessary.

The Infrastructure Improvement Program

The commission's recommendations became the basis for the city's Infrastructure Improvement Program and were largely implemented. Among these recommendations were catch-up spending for prompt construction of the Cornell pumping station (needed to better match the patterns of supply and demand in the city) and strong support for the previously recommended construction of the Cincinnati Water Works' activated granulated carbon treatment facility (at the California Water Treatment Plant) to remove organic carbon contaminants (i.e., pesticides and other chemical residues). This facility, with a treatment capacity of 270 million gallons per day and on-site regeneration of the carbon filters, was proposed to provide, words of in the commission report, the "safest affordable water from an industrial river source."

Another substantial action recommended was the replacement of electrical systems that power and control flood protection works in the Mill Creek Valley, which bisects the city and contains a significant portion of the city's industrial activity. The valley is also the location of the Metropolitan Sewer District's Mill Creek (Gest Street) Wastewater Treatment Plant, which provides secondary treatment for 70 percent of the city's sanitary and industrial

---

[13]Experience has led city staff to wish that a less complex formula had been developed.

wastes, by using activated sludge, anaerobic digestion, belt press sludge watering and incineration, and effluent chlorination. (Ash, trucked to a county landfill, can be used for daily cover in landfill operations.) In the same vicinity, a viaduct serving one of the city's more heavily used roads crosses the U.S. Army Corps of Engineers' Mill Creek Project, a flood control facility begun some 40 years ago. The severely deteriorated viaduct deck and structure required imposition of vehicle weight limitations. The city and the Corps have had to work together to ensure the continuity of traffic flow during both the design and construction of the Mill Creek Project and the viaduct's rehabilitation.

A notable exception to the record of successful implementation was the proposed construction of an incinerator and electrical co-generation facility for municipal solid waste management. Known to be controversial, the incinerator was nevertheless included in the commission's recommendations because, in the commissioners' view, it was the best solution to the city's solid waste problems. The recommendation and subsequent activities to implement that recommendation aroused strong local community opposition, centered in the neighborhood where the facility was to be located, [14] which the city council chose not to override. Defeat of the incinerator forced a complete change of the city's waste management strategy to the current emphasis on composting and recycling being pursued by DPW's newly formed Solid Waste Management Division (another of the commission's recommendations).

A budgeting and progress-monitoring process was established, with a major focus on how to control effectively the substantial increases in spending, over a relatively short period of time, required by the program's funding provisions. City staff prepared an implementation plan that included projections of budgets, staffing needs, and performance measures to be used in monitoring activity on the infrastructure improvement program. The task—and

---

[14]The location was the site of an older incineration facility that had for some years been out of service. Neighbors associated the soot, noise, and other nuisance of that previous operation with the proposed new operation.

the city budgeting process, in general—is made complex by the relatively large number of enterprise funds that have been established for specific restricted purposes. This complexity is an area to which the Smale commission did not give extensive attention.

The early stages of program implementation required careful planning and project management to coordinate and accomplish the large number of actions that individually seemed minor but had critical impact on the ability of the city to meet the program's spending requirements. The engineering staff often underestimated the time and effort required to complete administrative tasks on the critical path. For example, the commission recommended that consultants be used to reduce the need for city staff increases, but some new city contracting staff nevertheless had to be trained and able to deal effectively with consultants and contractors before the levels of construction activity could be raised substantially. Many easements and small parcels of property had to be acquired for rights of way, and DPW's direct costs for administrative actions (e.g., appraisal and negotiating fees) frequently exceeded the payment to the property owner. City agencies often had little basis for allocating indirect costs incurred in the program's execution. The city's mapping and administrative information systems also had to be upgraded substantially, although one of the Smale commission's recommendations—to develop a computerized geographic information system—is now being implemented and should make program management easier in the future.

City staff prepare performance reports, initially at six-month intervals and now annually, on progress in implementing the infrastructure improvement program. These reports to the city council were also reviewed by the Smale commission, which was not officially disbanded until 1991. The Cincinnati Business Committee, a continuing group of business leaders (not the same as the Smale Infrastructure Commission) agreed to continue this informal monitoring of the program's progress. The council and the business community may undertake a more formal fifth-year progress review and assessment.

71

How Representative Is the Cincinnati Experience?

Although not specifically included in the Infrastructure Commission's recommendations, refurbishment of the Ault Park Pavilion and the Union Terminal are symbolic of many of the special features of Cincinnati's experience. The Ault Park Pavilion, initially dedicated in 1930 on a scenic hilltop in one of the city's many parks, housed a restaurant and hosted dancing to live bands under the stars until the early 1960s. The limestone building and gardens suffered some two decades of neglect and vandalism, but have been restored as an important neighborhood and citywide amenity. The Union Terminal railroad station was opened in 1933 but was used for less than four decades before passenger rail traffic was terminated in 1972. (Limited Amtrak service has recently been reintroduced.) The station has been converted into the Museum Center at Cincinnati Union Terminal, housing a variety of displays on Cincinnati's natural and cultural history and attracting national acclaim for the quality of both the physical renewal and the museum operations.

Both projects may be seen to symbolize a community that has assessed the value of its physical assets and acted to maximize the return on those assets. Community representatives praise the Smale commission process for building community interest in these infrastructure assets. The community was willing to accept business leadership in this matter[15] and had a wealth of such leadership to draw upon. For many in the community, the orange barrels used as safety barriers in highway and street construction have become a widespread symbol of progress, and infrastructure investment is viewed as sending the "right signals" about Cincinnati's future. The committee found it difficult to assess the extent to which such attitudes and resources may be so abundantly available and effectively mobilized in other communities.

---

[15]Some participants, reflecting on the experience, acknowledge that a broader range of participants in the process might have been beneficial, even to the extent of achieving acceptance of the recommended incinerator project.

Figure 3-D

Cincinnati's Ault Park Pavilion was renovated in 1992 and returned to service as a popular place for strolling and a center for community recreation. Parks, open space, and such public facilities are likely to become increasingly important as elements of infrastructure.

At the same time, the margin of victory for the city's tax increase was small. Less effective strategies and leadership might have failed to achieve that victory. In addition, few cities own interstate freight rail lines or other already productive commercial assets. In such aspects, the financial arrangements of Cincinnati's program will be replicable in only a few communities.

Implementation of the Infrastructure Improvement Program, while administratively challenging, has benefited from the nation's and region's recessionary economic conditions that reduced total construction demand, intensified competition among contractors, and yielded lower bids for city projects. The program's administrators have been able to exceed most of the program's performance targets.

Extracting More General Principles

Notwithstanding such singular elements of success, Cincinnati's experience offers valuable insights for developing local programs and addressing national infrastructure policy:

• Individual leadership makes a crucial difference. The public works professionals had a clear vision of what was needed and maintained this vision in working with the community during strategy development and implementation. The community was organized under effective leadership by both elected officials and outside interests. The Smale commission, following on the results of the earlier Phillips committee's conclusions, provided a clearly defined way for this leadership to be exercised.

• Intimately involving community leadership—the business community in this case, but other institutions might be key in other communities—in the process of needs review was an important step. Development of a strategy for this involvement was crucial to the success of the program. There must be mutual respect of the participants for one another's competence and motives for the coalition of interests to form and work effectively. In addition, the coalition brings into the process important skills and judgments that public works and public administration professionals alone infrequently possess.

• Bringing the problems of infrastructure and the issues of how to deal with those problems to the voters' attention is a substantial challenge that must be met continuously, from early planning through strategy development and as implementation proceeds. The public must be kept apprised of progress, and must be able to see and understand that progress. Communication—in this case, through an effective media campaign and numerous neighborhood meetings—is a crucial element in program development and implementation.

• It is possible to deal with infrastructure as an entire system supporting community activity. Cincinnati's business community and voters recognized the importance of the whole, even while questioning the configuration of specific parts (e.g., the incinerator debate), and accepted the notion that the Infrastructure Improvement Program is "building Cincinnati's future" (the phrased used on project signage and progress reports).

• The process of dealing with infrastructure problems takes years. The community must have a mechanism for ensuring continuity in developing an understanding of its problems, formulating an effective program, and implementing that program. In Cincinnati, the highly professional city staff and a business community habituated to community service combined effectively to provide this continuity.

• The earlier work of the Phillips committee and the Cincinnati Business Committee's proposed midterm review of the Infrastructure Improvement Program are, in effect, community "peer reviews" of the work of city staff. These peer reviews may be an helpful tool for building mutual respect, defining common goals, and enhancing government staff's ability to identify and implement realistic infrastructure strategy.

• The importance of facility maintenance—and the costly consequences of its neglect—are clearly demonstrated. More than half of the Smale commission's recommendations involved catch-up expenditures.

• Inadequate understanding and respect for natural features—topography, geotechnical factors, hydrology, and growing conditions for plants (i.e., biotic communities)—have allowed development in Cincinnati, as in many other cities, to occur in patterns that have increased the costs and reduced the performance of infrastructure. Improved understanding of and respect for these features facilitate development of more efficient and environmentally less damaging urban patterns and infrastructures.

• The need for data to support infrastructure system planning and management had been underestimated, with the result that both the SMU and the Infrastructure Improvement Program were hampered by a lack of data for their implementation efforts. The development and maintenance of accurate, comprehensive, and current geographic information, in a readily and economically accessible system, may constitute one of the single most cost-effective steps a community can take toward addressing its infrastructure problems.

BOSTON, MASSACHUSETTS

The Committee on Infrastructure held its third workshop colloquium in Boston, Massachusetts, on August 31 and September 1 and 2, 1992. The workshop was scheduled to coincide with the 1992 International Public Works Congress and Exposition of the American Public Works Association. During the committee's meeting, members met with city and state government officials and members of community groups, visited several major projects, and observed various elements of the city's infrastructure.

Background

Capital of one of the original 13 colonies and an early commercial center, Boston is one of the nation's oldest and most historic cities. Over the years, the city has repeatedly demonstrated a willingness to consider new visions and remake itself, while seeking to preserve its most important historic landmarks.

Well established as a city by the time of the Revolution, Boston occupied a small area—almost an island—on the Shawmut Peninsula, joined to the mainland by a narrow neck of land. Filling of the coves and tidal flats within the Charles River Basin and the harbor surrounding this peninsula has added more than 3,200 acres to the original 785-acre area of the central city.

Boston's initial location and the region's geometry combined to encourage formation of a strongly radial pattern of arterial roads, with relatively weak interconnections between radials. Large-scale filling of an old milling pond extended the city's northern edge early in the nineteenth century, under a plan laid out by noted architect Charles Bullfinch. The "Bullfinch Triangle," a road pattern created by this plan, with Haymarket Square at its apex, responded in some degree to the radial pattern and survived intact for more than a century before being progressively obliterated by such projects as the initial Central Artery Scheme of the 1950s.

The Back Bay residential and commercial area is a product of another landfill operation of some 40 years' duration. The 1859 state legislation authorizing the filling and annexation of the new lands to the city of Boston included provision of funds for the construction of a major sewer across the lands that emptied into the Charles River. Included also was designation of land for a public garden adjacent to the Common, removing the possibility that land might be sold by the city for home sites.

Frederick Law Olmsted's late nineteenth century system of parks, the Emerald Necklace designed to provide for the physical and spiritual well-being of the urban residents, built on two decades of preparation by advocates for such a system. Olmsted's successor, Charles Eliot, extended the concept to a regionwide open space network that is today a landmark of achievement in landscape architecture.

In recent decades, Boston's economy has dipped and rebounded into what some observers term the "Boston Renaissance." Beginning in the late 1960s with the construction of the new city hall and rebuilding of its surroundings, a chain of major projects marks the progress of development and redevelopment that have made Boston a city with a diversity of people, style, age, and use.

Public Transport, Public Involvement, and the Southwest Corridor

The diversity of Boston is reflected in the Southwest Corridor project, a relocation and extension of the MBTA's (Massachusetts Bay Transportation Authority) Orange Line and related urban design development started in 1979 and, despite completion of the transit line's construction, still evolving. Built on a right of way originally intended for an interstate highway, the corridor's rail and rapid transit facilities serve a large local and commuter population while providing parkland and other open space in several neighborhoods along a corridor 4.7 miles long, from downtown Boston to the community of Forest Hills.

The project is an end product of a history beginning with community anger and activism in the 1960s, aimed at stopping highway construction that had disrupted strong ethnic communities, and the conflict with construction industry workers whose jobs would be threatened if highway construction were curtailed. Participants in the discussions about the city's transportation realized that a way had to be found to give something to all sides. In 1970, the governor of Massachusetts halted highway construction and ordered a complete review of all aspects of transportation for the Boston region. After this review, which included then-unprecedented levels of public involvement and review of plan alternatives, the decision was made to improve rail and transit facilities and local and arterial street systems. The transfer of interstate highway funds to other uses, enabled by the 1973 Federal Highway Act, was the first such major transfer in the nation, made possible by the coincidence of what some observers characterize as an unusually talented and committed set of government officials at local, state, and national levels.

The planning process that evolved in this environment involved the extensive participation of community groups of many types, from residents of neighborhoods located along the right of way to labor union representatives. An unusual coalition of interests evolved as this planning proceeded.

The planning team worked closely with neighborhood people to define the nature of appropriate urban design responses to the rail line and stations that would be placed in their areas. The socioeconomic characteristics of these areas spanned a broad range. One technique used, for example, was to ask neighborhood children to draw and discuss what they would like to see in the neighborhood, and then use that information in the landscape design of parks constructed on decking over the rail line.

The plan that emerged for the Southwest Corridor replaced the highway with a transit line, as well as extensive parks and station area development. An antiquated elevated section of the old MBTA line was relocated and placed in an open-cut, below-grade right of way, subsequently covered over by decking in segments to provide playgrounds and a stronger link between previously highway-divided neighborhoods. Existing rail lines were accommodated, protecting commuter rail service.

Members of the planning team felt that a key point in the planning was acceptance by both elected and transportation agency staff officials that the result of planning would be a complete community redevelopment project, rather than simply a transit line extension. For example, a series of drawings was prepared to illustrate to design engineers the sorts of architectural and visual conditions that should be provided in each area, and how such conditions would contribute to the solution of neighborhood problems beyond those of the transit line alone. The enhanced urban design character along the corridor is credited with stimulating private investment in it and convincing residents to turn toward the corridor in their private planning and design.

An element of the project's success has been demonstrated in the community's response to governmental budgetary problems of the early 1990s. Faced with reduced budgets, the Metropolitan District Commission, which is responsible for maintenance of the

Figure 3-E

This approach to downtown Boston—lined with houses and small shops, and passing through flower and vegetable gardens, parks and playgrounds—is built above the Metropolitan Boston Transportation Authority's Orange Line. Much of the rapid rail transit line is, in turn, located in a right of way cleared in the 1960s for construction of a segment of the interstate highway system. Community questioning of the balance and distribution of costs and benefits of this segment led to the nation's first major reprogramming of federal transportation funds from one mode to another.

park system constructed on decking over the transit line, reduced maintenance activities. Residents of the South End who live along the corridor "adopted" sections of the line and took on cleanup activities in their sections.

Building the Central Artery/Third Harbor Tunnel

Also resulting from the review process that spurred the Southwest Corridor were plans to build a third tunnel under Boston Harbor and to reconstruct the elevated Central Artery underground through Boston's downtown area. Management of these two projects was subsequently combined, creating the nation's largest transportation project, estimated to total some $6.5 billion in construction costs (1992 dollars).

The combined Central Artery/Third Harbor Tunnel (CA/THT) project is designed to relieve serious traffic congestion, complete a linking of the Massachusetts Turnpike to Boston's Logan Airport, and remove a visual and physical barrier dividing the downtown area. The project is expected to generate no more traffic than would have been anticipated without this construction. The Central Artery, originally designed to carry 75,000 vehicles per day, now serves 190,000. The new facility is planned to accommodate 220,000 vehicles daily, and will divert thousands of vehicle trips from downtown routes by providing them with direct airport access.

Current traffic is heavily congested for 8 hours per day, a figure that is projected to grow to 14 hours a day by the year 2010 unless action is taken. The tunnel to the airport is designed to improve goods movement by serving truck traffic that now must use the badly congested existing tunnels or neighborhood streets in East Boston. Utilities along the Central Artery, now scattered throughout the area, will be consolidated into a few corridors adjacent to the roadway and in designated crossover corridors.

In addition to traffic relief, the project is forecast to generate 5,000 construction jobs and 10,000 additional jobs in Boston and elsewhere. Employment generation, along with the consequent support of organized labor in the political decision-making process, was an important contributor to the coalition building apparent in the CA/THT as well as the Southwest Corridor projects. Some residents and other observers question the wisdom of such major investment in highways, and attribute the decision to make this investment to political and business interests. Federal funding was in fact provided as part of the congressional action to override a presidential veto of a major highway bill.

While such questions concerning the project's planning are still discussed, the CA/THT is now under construction, and the management team's primary goal is to maintain progress and thus control the costs and adverse impact of this construction. Continuing opposition from some segments of the community requires the management team's steady attention to avoiding disruption. To this end, the team brings together sound engineering knowledge, good negotiating skills, and tough litigation experience to demonstrate that it can discuss issues of the project's implementation but is prepared to fight if necessary to maintain progress.

A threat to progress that has influenced other highway projects is action from environmental groups, and the Sierra Club has expressed solid opposition to the CA/THT projects. However, other environmental groups have seemingly accepted that gains such as the new open space being developed and the projected reduction in air polluting emissions render the project, on balance, an asset to the community, whether viewed as the last activity of the interstate highway era or the first of a new wave of urban investment.

The Federal Highway Administration is viewing the project as one of a new generation of transport improvements with fully integrated attention to environmental concerns. Of the estimated $6.5 billion cost of the total project, some 10 percent will be spent to mitigate or avoid adverse environmental consequences or to enhance the environment. In many cases the actions taken to further environmental aims make good economic sense as well. For example, the "fish startle" program intended to reduce fish kills during dredging and blasting operations avoids 70-day project delays that would otherwise have been necessary during the fish migration season in Boston Harbor.

Massachusetts Water Resource Authority "Turning the Tide on Pollution"

Adverse impact and its prevention or mitigation are topics that assume major proportions when discussion turns to the construction project at Deer Island, known as the Boston Harbor Cleanup or more recently as "Turning the Tide on Pollution." The wastewater and water system project, with a projected 10-year cost of $6 billion to $7 billion, is a court-ordered response to what some people view as the Boston region's years of neglect that had turned Boston Harbor into one of the nation's most polluted and persistent violations of federal Clean Water Act (CWA) requirements. Poor maintenance and inadequate capacity had made even the existing treatment plants almost totally ineffective. Funding for improvements, politically controlled, was not forthcoming.

Communities along the shoreline were exposed to the pollution and associated odor and health hazard of the millions of tons of raw sewage dumped regularly into the harbor. In 1982 the city solicitor for Quincy, one of those communities, filed suit in the state court against the Metropolitan District Commission (MDC), the responsible state agency, seeking relief. A regional environmental group filed suit the following year in federal court against the MDC and the U.S. Environmental Protection Agency (EPA). Court action was felt to be needed because (1) there was no information available on the existing plant's performance or current environmental conditions, (2) no local constituencies for action had yet formed, and (3) there was no political leadership for action. In addition, the state's elected officials continued to neglect to provide for the MDC's funding needs.

The court provided leadership and brought groups together. However, agreements reached under the first suit failed to have significant effect, and a consensus of the parties to the related discussions was that a new entity should take over MDC sewage functions. A combination of actions by the two courts and the EPA forced the state legislature to establish the Massachusetts Water Resources Authority (MWRA), which is now responsible for supplying water and sewer services in 61 cities and towns, in the Boston area.

Almost immediately after the MWRA was created, the EPA in early 1985 filed suit against the authority for alleged violations of the CWA. By the end of the year, a court-ordered schedule of action had been established to bring the MWRA into compliance with the Act. This schedule has subsequently been modified several times in negotiations with EPA, nearby communities, and other parties to the suits.

A major element in the schedule of action is the consolidation and upgrading of sewage treatment operations at the MWRA's Deer Island facility, where a large secondary treatment plant is now under construction. That project, currently estimated to cost $1.5 billion, includes a 9.5-mile, 24.5-foot-diameter, hard rock tunnel under Boston Harbor to discharge treated waste through 55 diffusers located 110 feet under the surface of Massachusetts Bay. Local environmental groups and residents of communities on Cape Cod are questioning the potential impact of the project on aquatic life, while the scientific community is deeply divided on the environmental benefits and cost-effectiveness of secondary treatment for coastal waste disposal.

Hence, the MWRA management team is concerned, like the CA/THT team, about timely progress as a primary goal. In the agency's view, delay will only add to the project's already high costs, payment of which has multiplied the water and sewer rates of households in the region to levels that are now among the highest in the nation. Although some 87 percent of the estimated costs of the Central Artery/Third Harbor Tunnel project are federally funded, 90 percent of the estimated costs of the Deer Island project will be local. Authority staff report that no provision is yet being made to ensure the availability of adequate funds for facility maintenance in the future.

The context provided by the court's involvement has required that many alternatives for each major decision be considered, and the judge in the case has tended toward selecting the more difficult options (politically or administratively) to achieve environmental benefits. Although other approaches might in principle yield even greater benefits (e.g., several satellite treatment facilities rather than the large Deer Island plant), the practical feasibility of these options is questionable (e.g., neighborhood resistance to the siting of several satellite plants). Nevertheless, little if any consideration seems to have been given to conservation efforts, such as replacement of plumbing fixtures in the region, that might reduce the need for a major treatment plant.

How Representative Is the Boston Experience?

The Boston experience, reflected in the Southwest Corridor, Central Artery/Third Harbor Tunnel, and Harbor Cleanup projects, brings to the forefront the question of national interests in local infrastructures, primarily because of their large scale and use of federal resources. In this case, "resources" must be broadly viewed as encompassing the judicial and administrative systems, as well as flows of funding.

Scale is of course very significant. The estimated combined cost of the two ongoing projects, $14 billion, even when distributed over a 10-year period, is a significant fraction of U.S. spending on infrastructure. The allocation of those costs among the residents and businesses of the Boston region, the state of Massachusetts, and the nation as a whole is a matter of national importance, as the histories of the three projects illustrate. However, this huge scale necessarily limits the applicability of the Boston experience.

The projects also illustrate the trade-offs to be made among services provided by infrastructure, the jobs created by infrastructure investment, and the environmental consequences of construction and long-term operation of the systems. In both the CA/THT project and the Southwest Corridor, jobs were a key issue in building the coalitions that determined that those projects would

Figure 3-F

Infrastructure construction projects are often among the largest and most complex and costly civil engineering undertakings. Operations of this dredge working on Boston's Third Harbor Tunnel project adjust to seasonal fish migrations as well as tides and storms.

proceed. The Central Artery, projected to reduce congestion without increasing traffic volume over what would otherwise have been expected, could be portrayed as likely to enhance the environment as well as improve transport. Such trade-offs are inherent to all infrastructure investment and operation, regardless of scale.

Extracting More General Principles

Thus, the Boston experience is in many ways unique. Nevertheless, it yields more general principles that may be useful both in dealing with infrastructure matters elsewhere and in understanding how national policy shapes local infrastructure:

• Very large projects "crowd out" and force deferral of other smaller but possibly beneficial projects, particularly over the term during which high "carrying costs" must be borne. Powerful political forces tend to favor larger projects or programs, which suggests that smaller projects will be more appealing if grouped into some credible unifying framework.

• A long-term perspective for financing the maintenance and repair of major facilities is needed. The apparent lack of such perspective in Boston's major projects is a serious flaw suggesting that these major new investments will not yield their highest possible return. This lesson was clearly demonstrated in the Cincinnati experience.

• The long gestation period of large projects increases their costs and poses inherent obstacles to their ultimate completion. These large projects are often, as one observer termed them, "faith-based" investments. Nevertheless, the Boston experience demonstrates that such projects, once they gain a critical mass, possess a momentum that carries them through changes in political leadership and economic cycles.

• The availability of funds earmarked for some purposes may give particular agencies or infrastructure modes considerable advantage, sometimes—to the extent that total resources are limited—at the expense of other programs and projects. The progress of the Central Artery/Third Harbor Tunnel project is made possible in a period of record government deficits by the availability of earmarked highway gasoline tax revenues.

• Economic growth is a significant element of success in developing the political coalitions needed to accomplish major shifts in infrastructure policy. When all sides can come out better in the end, it is easier to convince them to join together for a common purpose. The need for jobs and the advantages to local businesses combined to facilitate local political support for Boston's large projects.

REFERENCES

Bureau of the Census. 1992. Statistical Abstract of the United States, Appendix II. Washington, D.C.: U.S. Department of Commerce.

Dibner, D.R., and A.C. Lemer. 1992. The Role of Public Agencies in Fostering New Technology and Innovation in Building. Washington, D.C.: National Academy Press.

Dolin, E.J. 1992. Environment 34(6):7-33.

Johnson, D. 1991. Arid economy, desert states thrive. New York Times May 13: A1.

Krieger, A., and L.J. Green. 1985. Past Futures: Two Centuries of Imagining Boston. Cambridge, Mass.: Harvard Graduate School of Design.

World Almanac and Book of Facts. 1992. New York: Pharos Books.

4

PRINCIPLES FOR ACTION ON INFRASTRUCTURE

In their visits to Phoenix, Cincinnati, and Boston, committee members observed local conditions and talked to private citizens and to representatives of the business communities and governments, who were grappling with issues of infrastructure development and management. Each community is unique, as the committee's observations show well, and uniqueness is reflected in a community's infrastructure. Location determines the characteristics of geology and soil, hydrology, topography, vegetation, and climate with which the infrastructures must contend. The economic and social makeup of the community shapes the demand for the infrastructure's services, in terms of prices willingly paid as well as types and levels of services desired, and the performance levels that are judged to be minimally acceptable. The history of the community establishes patterns of physical development, institutional and political relationships, and attitudes that influence what can be practically achieved in the infrastructure's development and management.

Perhaps the most important lesson the committee observed is that the local community must be responsible for determining its own priorities. Communities will be most successful in building and maintaining their infrastructure if they can devise mechanisms enabling these priorities to be determined with minimal waste of time, money, and human effort. These mechanisms have something to do with effective application and management of the technology of infrastructure within the context of the social, political, and economic forces of the community that this infrastructure serves.

THREE KEY PRINCIPLES FOR ACTION

From its experience, the committee extracted three broad principles for dealing with local infrastructure issues, principles that can lead toward "win-win" situations in which parties with potentially opposing interests seek a way to resolve a conflict such that all parties gain. These principles are complex and multi-faceted, but can be simply stated: geography matters; the paradigm is broadening; value the "public" in public works.

Finding solutions to a community's infrastructure problems that are unambiguously win-win may be impossible, but experience suggests that the right strategy—one tailored to the specific character of the community—can make the difference. Specific examples observed by the committee in Boston, Cincinnati, and Phoenix support and demonstrate these principles, but such cases can be found in other areas as well.

At their core, these principles represent a return to what works: good planning, good management, and good community relations. Within the context of practices of the past several decades, applying these principles means a shift toward a broader view and broader participation in the infrastructure system planning, development, and management.

Principle 1: Geography Matters

The specific physical, social, economic, and environmental characteristics of a region should be the primary factors shaping that region's infrastructure investment and management. National policy must deal effectively with local concerns, allowing solutions to be tailored to the natural environment, social patterns, and locally assessed needs and aspirations of the region.

Current infrastructure technology enables us to move water uphill, cut steeper slopes on the land than would be found in nature, and take other actions in opposition to natural forms and forces. As experience makes increasingly clear, such actions, although possible, are not necessarily good. Cincinnati's need for retaining walls and the flooding and drainage problems plaguing some neighborhoods are the results of development with limited regard for natural drainage and slope conditions. Phoenix's dependence on distant water sources is a result of growth allowed to exceed locally available supplies.[16]

Such observations are a reminder that infrastructure should be designed and managed to **respect the natural features** (e.g., drainage, geology) and social structure of the community and to be compatible with these features.[17] The history of Boston's transit extensions shows that there should be **respect** for **the social and cultural character of a region,** as well as compatibility. These **natural, social, and cultural features are connected** in complex ways that should shape the region's infrastructure.

Good decision making should be based on good information, but the committee's experience demonstrates that frequently the data needed to support thorough analysis of infrastructure problems and alternative solutions are not available. Many cities, especially older ones like Boston, do not know the location or condition of many of their infrastructure facilities. Many cities have only limited information on subsurface conditions, natural drainage, and

---

[16]Similar statements might be made about transportation corridors passing through established communities, the source of Boston's Southeast Corridor experience. Over the past decades, federal programs that made funds available for such investments have had major impact in shaping metropolitan development but have often neglected the diverse social, economic, and physical character of local geography.

[17]In the summer of 1993, as one reviewer of the committee's work pointed out, severe flooding of cities and towns in the Mississippi and Missouri River valleys illustrated graphically the importance of this respect.

other factors with which they must contend when developing facility plans or management policies.

To effect a true respect for geography in all its aspects, local authorities must **collect and maintain good data** to support effective decision making **and good documentation** of the bases and consequences of decisions. Increasingly powerful and lower-cost computer-based geographic information systems (GISs) will facilitate data management and documentation.[18]

Principle 2: The Paradigm Is Broadening

The future goal of infrastructure management must be to change the paradigm of independent management of the many elements of infrastructure and in its place incorporate effective recognition of infrastructure as a multimodal and multipurpose system—a stream of services—as well as an armature of community development. Infrastructure facilities require land and capital, two resources invariably in shorter supply as cities or regions mature and grow. Such limited resources should be used as efficiently as possible, considering all elements of the system together.

Phoenix's solid waste transfer facility demonstrates how infrastructure facility planning, design, and management can seek to **deliver multiple services.** Boston's transportation planning shows how communities can **be flexible in allocating resources within the whole system to suit local conditions,** always examining

---

[18]Development of metropolitan GISs is hampered by missing data and by diversity in the level of detail, age, format, and reliability of data that are available. In addition, researchers and competing vendors have struggled to define common formats for data management. However, many areas are working to consolidate their data resources. The committee did not directly review such work, but rather drew on the knowledge of its members. For further discussion, see National Research Council (NRC, 1993).

multiple solutions for each problem and taking a long term perspective in decision making that extends beyond the traditional 15- to 30-year design service life or bond financing horizon.

Increasing the investment in infrastructure, although often necessary and appropriate, is not sufficient by itself to solve a region's or the nation's problems. Serious questions must be faced about the technological range, investment scale, and financial costs of alternatives for construction and reconstruction, the role of resource conservation as a management and investment strategy, the frequently neglected long-term costs of ownership of facilities, and the impact of changing regional and global economies on the region's and nation's ability or willingness to pay for infrastructure's services.

Maintenance is a key case in point. Cincinnati's "crisis" stemmed from neglect of maintenance. As Cincinnati's Infrastructure Commission found, **new systems for monitoring and maintaining infrastructure condition and performance at appropriate levels are needed,** systems that are less susceptible to shifting political forces. Boston's current investment boom may lead to maintenance cost crises in the future.

To the extent that national policies support infrastructure, these policies should be shifted from a narrow focus on transportation, water resources, or other single elements of the infrastructure system. **National infrastructure policies and programs should be structured to foster a new paradigm that enables appropriate trade-offs among infrastructure modes and brings together the interests of diverse regions within a context of equity among cities and regions.** Examination of a range of alternatives to any proposed infrastructure development, always good practice and required in some cases when federal funding is involved, should be done from a multimodal and services-based perspective.

Overall, a shift in outlook is needed from "catch-up" to forward-looking development. Achieving this shift will require more effective consideration of the life-cycle consequences of infrastructure decisions, and the possible shifting of technologies and of economic and social priorities that can warrant demand management and decommissioning, as well as service expansion and the development of new infrastructures.

This new paradigm must be presented and refined through the education of infrastructure professionals and policy makers. **Infrastructure professionals need a broader and more integrative educational experience** that will enable them to communicate effectively with the public and policy makers, as well as manage the infrastructure system. Phoenix's experience demonstrates why policy makers should **give greater recognition to the enabling value of infrastructure, by promoting and rewarding innovation in infrastructure technology and management.**

This educational experience should aim also to make these professionals more responsive to the very real mismatch that typically occurs in infrastructure development and use among those who receive benefits from the system's services, those who pay most directly for those services, and those who suffer losses. The history of Boston's Southwest Corridor development, as told to the committee during its visit, highlights the social and economic factors this mismatch often entails.

Research and development contribute to our understanding of the services that infrastructure can provide and the options for providing these services more effectively, and may lead to innovation if results are transferred into practice. **Local demonstrations are a valuable form of research and development that should be used to verify and disseminate new technology.**

Principle 3: Value The "Public" In Public Works

Infrastructure encompasses more than public works, but nevertheless is intended essentially to serve the public. However, for a number of reasons outlined in earlier chapters and observable in Phoenix, Cincinnati, and Boston, the development and management of infrastructure are the realm of politicians and professionals, civil engineers, urban planners, and specialists in related law and finance. Although these professionals have served the nation well in providing the United States with what is arguably the world's best infrastructure, the committee's observations in this study as well as committee members' broader experience illustrate that improvements can be made by introducing new ways of thinking about the problems of infrastructure.

These improvements are visible in the civic pride in Cincinnati's renovation, the neighborhood care maintained in Boston's Southwest Corridor, and the public's ultimate satisfaction with Phoenix's Squaw Peak Parkway. Other professions and the community at large—urban designers, artists, school teachers, and children—can make solid contributions by asking questions that spark rethinking of conventional solutions to problems and by providing input to infrastructure development and management. Ways should be sought to involve new people and diverse groups whose interests have previously been underrepresented in these processes.

Specific efforts must be made also to involve the broader public in infrastructure decisionmaking. These efforts, increasingly required by statute[19], are as likely as not to be viewed by responsible officials as burdensome or irrelevant. The public antagonism, opposition, and consequent project delays that this separation of the public from public works generates are visible in the cases the committee reviewed.

Visible as well is the value of early and steady involvement of the public in infrastructure decisionmaking. This involvement can and should occur at various levels—from the personal and intimate participation of individuals in construction of the Thomas Road Overpass in Phoenix, to the many neighborhood meetings held in Cincinnati to discuss priorities and needs, to the large- scale public replanning of Boston's highway system.

Effective public involvement and broad intersectoral and interdisciplinary partnerships in infrastructure development and management are needed to apply the broader paradigm of flexible delivery of multiple services. As Cincinnati's experience

---

[19]The National Environmental Policy Act, which became federal law in 1969, was an early and major force for full disclosure of government plans for infrastructure development.

Figure 4-A

In Boston's South End neighborhood, matching the design of the subway transit's ventilation tower to the style of adjacent residences converted a potential eyesore and source of community resentment to an attractive and accepted addition to the urban landscape.

showed, inclusion by the community of broad representation of users and neighbors of infrastructure within these partnerships strengthens decision making. Such involvement can help to resolve the conflicts and inequities associated with infrastructure's development and operations.

The importance of effective leadership in dealing with issues of infrastructure is a direct corollary of broad public involvement and introduction of new ways of thinking into the decision-making process. Disagreements and disputes will inevitably arise, often over questions which there are only opinions but no correct answers, and leadership will be needed to reach resolution.

Although this leadership is often seemingly embodied in a single individual such as Cincinnati's John Smale or Massachusetts' governor William F. Weld, invariably these individuals are supported by many others who exercise leadership in their communities and on teams of professionals. Efforts to enable and even encourage this leadership to develop within all parts of the community can help to ensure that broad participation and new ideas are effective.

All three cities visited by the committee showed that to build leadership and effectiveness, the people responsible for approving infrastructure development (i.e., voters) need to be better informed to judge matters of infrastructure technology and its impact on the economy, the environment, and the general quality of life. More than two decades of public discussion in Boston produced a population singularly well prepared to discuss infrastructure, and the educational components of Phoenix's 27th Avenue waste management facility seem likely to produce similar benefits over the longer term. Such an educated public is a source of leadership and new ideas, and cannot help but enhance the community's ability to manage and develop its infrastructure more effectively. **Public education is an essential element of future infrastructure management.**

Sometimes formal mechanisms are needed to bring the knowledge of an educated public and broader range of professionals to bear on specific problems. One such mechanism is periodic review of infrastructure management and planning by a knowledgeable group of people who are not otherwise involved in the decision-making process. Such a group, sometimes termed a "jury" in architectural design practice or "peer reviewers" in many professional circles, contributes by asking questions and in effect testing the assumptions and conclusions of the decisionmakers. In this role, it does not so much pass judgment as test the validity and robustness of ongoing programs. The Cincinnati business community's reviews of municipal government and the infrastructure program are outstanding examples of this strategy at work. Infrastructure professionals should **include community peer review of plans and progress as a regular part of major infrastructure decisionmaking.** Such peer review can build the new coalitions of diverse interest groups that the broader paradigm will bring.

TOWARD NATIONAL POLICY AND BEYOND

A national perspective can bring together the interests of diverse regions. Only at the national level are there means for maintaining equity among cities and regions and for fostering the structures in local government to support the new management paradigm of infrastructure as a system of services. National infrastructure policy can address effectively—in a way that is not possible at local levels alone—the balance of resources applied among infrastructure modes and between infrastructure and other issues of national interest (e.g., national security, industrial competitiveness, medical care, and AIDS research). However, there is presently no delineated statement of national policy toward infrastructure, but rather a complex and often conflicting collection of laws, regulations, standards, and programs that address separately the various modes and their impacts.

National strategic interests arise from infrastructure's pervasive influence on our economic productivity, our environment, and ultimately our quality of life. In its 1990 report on state and local public works financing and management, the Office of Technology Assessment (OTA) discussed the gap between these national and local concerns, which is nowhere more evident than in the responsibilities and regulations for environmental protection and remediation. OTA (1990) termed environmental problems

> an excruciating modern dilemma: the need for better stewardship of our air, water, and land resources has become critical due to many of the very practices that have helped our Nation grow and flourish. Land use and transportation patterns that fostered economic development and personal mobility in the past now embody environmental issues that will require changes beyond our current ability to conceive in industry operations and personal living and travel habits. State and local officials in major urban and high-growth areas understand that congested highways and airports, substandard air quality, and inadequate solid waste and wastewater facilities make them less attractive to business. However, the changes needed to resolve the issues are so difficult and far reaching that they cannot be understood, developed, or implemented quickly, easily, or inexpensively.

National policy must deal effectively with the essentially local concerns of infrastructure, concerns that are closely tied to the specific characteristics of a region and intimately related to the region's environmental conditions. In their efforts to establish national standards and procedures, some federal infrastructure programs in the past have not dealt well with this need for local focus. For example, the interstate highway program generated substantial resistance in many cities as the urban links of the system approached design and construction. Phoenix and Boston revealed the vestiges of such resistance. There is evidence that enforcement of uniform national pollution standards may impose selectively very high infrastructure costs on some regions where other ways might be found to accomplish environmental goals. Boston may again provide a case study. In all three cities, the evidence is seen of how failures to establish effective mechanisms for bringing the full costs of public goods such as clean air and water into local decision making may lead to suboptimal invest-ment and distortion of the infrastructure system.

The new Intermodal Surface Transportation Efficiency Act (ISTEA, popularly referred to as "ice tea") may be an exemplar of federal law that gives more effective recognition to local concerns. This 1991 legislation includes broad provisions for intermodal coordination and community planning that some professionals feel are likely to change in basic ways in which U.S. urban transpor-tation works. Nevertheless, ISTEA is still a transportation act and has little, if any, consequence for water supply, sewerage, tele-communications, and other elements of infrastructure.

The impact of national policies and programs across all infrastructure modes should be considered when new legislation is prepared and in reviewing what already exists. There is ample experience to demonstrate that funding or restricting water supply influences the perceived need for transportation, for example, and vice versa. If communities are to take an integrated, multimodal view in developing and managing their infrastructure, federal programs must be supportive.

A particularly important form of support is the federal funding of infrastructure research, development, and demonstration activities. Such agencies as the National Science Foundation, Department of Transportation, U.S. Army Corps of Engineers, and Environmental Protection Agency can and should foster cross-cutting research to improve local areas' capabilities for life-cycle management, condition monitoring and performance assessment, and information and system management. Such research can contribute to our understanding of infrastructure as a multimodel system and of the sources that system can provide. The research should include federally sponsored local demonstration projects, which experience has shown to be a valuable means for developing and disseminating innovation.

The absence of a clearly defined center of federal responsibility for infrastructure policy and programs makes coordination and concerted effort more difficult. Some observers suggest that a single agency with sweeping responsibilities is needed to ensure that federal investments are made efficiently and effectively. However, the committee does not recommend such strong centralization. Apart from the relatively brief existence of the Public Works Administration and other federal agencies created in response to the challenges of the Great Depression and two World Wars, no serious effort has been made to centralize responsibilities across infrastructure programs at national levels, and such an effort would conflict with long-standing institutional relationships. Resolving such conflict would be slow and difficult, and substantial centralization of executive authority might further limit communities' abilities to shape their infrastructure to meet unique needs.

Nevertheless, dealing effectively with the nation's infrastructure problems will require vision and leadership at all levels. Adequate infrastructure is a crucial element of the national enabling environment needed for increasing productivity and improving quality of life. Effective national policy can support that enabling environment by providing the framework for alleviating many of the problems our infrastructure faces.

Yet infrastructure is essentially local, and local differences will always require specific variations in facilities, management systems, and funding patterns. A supportive national policy environment must facilitate strategies for addressing issues of infrastructure to be applied locally--to paraphrase the often used phrase of resistance to infrastructure--in our own backyards.

REFERENCES

NRC (National Research Council). 1993. Toward a Coordinate Spatial Data Infrastructure for the Nation. Mapping Science Committee. Washington, D.C.: National Academy Press.
OTA (U.S. Congress, Office of Technology Assessment). 1990. Rebuilding the Foundations. Washington, D.C.: U.S. Government Printing Office.

APPENDIX A

BIOGRAPHICAL SKETCHES OF COMMITTEE MEMBERS AND STAFF COMMITTEE MEMBERS

ALBERT A. GRANT, P.E. has had more than 40 years of experience in the planning and engineering of public works infrastructure. Currently a consulting engineer specializing in transportation and infrastructure planning and management, he was formerly the Director of Transportation Planning, Washington Metropolitan Council of Governments (1966-1987); and Engineer and Chief Engineer, Office of Planning and Programming, District of Columbia (1949-1966). Mr. Grant was 1987-1988 National President of the American Society of Civil Engineers (ASCE) and the 1981 recipient of the ASCE's Harland Bartholomew Award "for outstanding contributions to the field of transportation and urban planning." He is the past Chairman of the American Association of Engineering Societies and was a director on the Accreditation Board for Engineering and Technology. He received his bachelor's degree in civil engineering from the Catholic University of America in 1948.

CLAIRE BARRETT is Special Assistant to the Executive Director of Massport, owner and operator of Logan Airport, Hanscom Field, the Port of Boston, and the Tobin Bridge. Until March 1991, she was the Director of Public Affairs for Boston's Central Artery/Third Harbor Tunnel Project, responsible for dissemination of information on all areas of the largest highway project in the U.S., from construction procedures to environmental and community issues; she formerly managed noise abatement and marketing programs at Logan Airport and served as director of the Massachusetts Bay Transportation Authority. She holds a master's degree in art history from the Institute of Fine Arts at New York University, and a bachelor's degree from Vassar College. She was the recipient of a Woodrow Wilson Fellowship for graduate study.

MICHAEL A. COHEN, Ph.D. is Chief, Urban Development Division, Infrastructure and Urban Development Department of the World Bank and, since 1972, has held a variety of positions in that organization in areas of urban development policy, water supply, housing, and project feasibility. He is author of *Learning by Doing: World Bank Lending for Urban Development, 1972-82*, and a major participant in shaping the bank's policies toward lending for urban infrastructure. Prior to joining the bank, he worked for the Urban Institute doing economic and financial analyses for the President's Commission on School Finance. He received his Ph.D. degree in political economy (1971) from the University of Chicago.

WILLIAM C. COLEMAN is President of Leggatt McCall Properties Management, Inc. Formerly, he was a managing director and New England Regional Manager of Public Finance for Smith Barney, Harris Upham & Co., and Director of Aviation of the Massachusetts Port Authority. He has served in several management and financial positions with the Commonwealth of Massachusetts and Massachusetts General Hospital. He received his B.A. and M.B.A. degrees from Harvard University.

ELLIS L. JOHNSON, Ph.D. teaches at the Georgia Institute of Technology at the School of Design and Systems Engineering and is a member of the research staff and a senior manager at IBM's T.J. Watson Research Center. He was formerly Assistant Professor, Yale University (1964-1967). He received his B.S. degree in mathematics from Georgia Institute of Technology (1960), and an M.A. in mathematics (1962) and Ph.D. in operations research (1965) from the University of California at Berkeley. Dr. Johnson is recipient of numerous awards and honors for his work, including the Lancaster Prize of the Operations Research Society of America, and the Dantzig Prize of the Mathematical Programming Society and the Society for International Applied Mathematics. He is a member of the National Academy of Engineering.

GORDON S. KINO, Ph.D. is Associate Dean of Engineering at Stanford University. He served as a member of the (NRC) Committee on Infrastructure Innovation and National Materials Advisory Board. He is a member of the National Academy of Engineering. He received his B.S. and M.S. degrees from the University of London, and his Ph.D. from Stanford University.

DAVID MARKS, Ph.D. is Director, Program in Environmental Engineering Education and Research, at the Massachusetts Institute of Technology. Widely recognized as an expert in water quality and hazardous systems management, he has served on several NRC committees and was chairman of the Office of Technology Assessment's Oversight Committee on Superfund. Dr. Marks received his B.S. degree in civil engineering (1962) and M.S. degree in environmental engineering (1964) from Cornell University, and his Ph.D. in environmental engineering (1969) from Johns

Hopkins University. He is a registered engineer in Massachusetts and New York, and a registered hydrologist with the American Institute of Hydrology.

WILLIAM REES MORRISH is Dayton Hudson Professor in Urban Design, Director, Design Center for American Urban Landscape (DC/AUL), an urban design research center in the College of Architecture and Landscape Architecture at the University of Minnesota. An architect and associate professor, he holds a B.Arch. from the University of California, Berkeley and an M.Arch. in urban design from the Harvard University Graduate School of Design. He is responsible for structuring DC/AUL as an independent, cross-disciplinary graduate program and research think tank that bridges both academic and community issues. Prior to assuming the directorship of DC/AUL, he was principal in the urban design firm CITYWEST, Inc., located in Los Angeles, specializing in the integration of public art, cultural planning, and public works development into urban design plans for American cities. He has taught at the University of Southern California, University of California, Berkeley—and Los Angeles, Tulane University, Morgan State University, and Harvard University.

JOSEPH C. PERKOWSKI, Ph.D. is Manager of the Advanced Civil Systems program in the Research and Development Department of Bechtel, responsible for the effective technical and business integration of new technological developments within the strategic plan of Bechtel Civil, Inc., the operating arm of Bechtel in the area of civil systems. He was formerly Staff Programs Manager of the Building Systems Company, a subsidiary of United Technologies Corporation (1982-1986); Vice President of Oxford Development Group, Ltd. (1979-1982); and Senior Research Officer in the Corporate Department of Environmental and Social Affairs at Petro-Canada. He holds a Ph.D. in environmental systems management from the Department of Civil Engineering at the Massachusetts Institute of Technology.

JANICE ELAINE PERLMAN, Ph.D. is Director, Mega-Cities Project of the Urban Research Center, and Adjunct Professor, Graduate School of Public Administration at New York University. Formerly the Director of Science and Public Policy Program, New York Academy of Sciences (1984-1987), as well as Assistant and Associate Professor, Department of City and Regional Planning, University of California, Berkeley (1973-1984) and Santa Cruz (1971-1973), she has served as a consultant to the World Bank, the U.S. Department of Housing and Urban Development, and U.S. Agency for International Development. Dr. Perlman received a B.A. degree, cum laude, in anthropology (1965) from Cornell University and Ph.D. in political science from the Massachusetts Institute of Technology. Widely traveled and published, she has served on the Board on Science and Technology for International Development.

105

SERGIO RODRIGUEZ, AICP is Assistant City Manager for the city of Miami, and Director of the Planning Department and the Building and Zoning Department. He is a former urban design coordinator and later chief planner for the Maryland-National Capital Parks and Planning Commission. He served in city planning and urban design positions in the Anne Arundel County Planning and Zoning Office, as well as several architectural and planning firms in the United States and Puerto Rico. He is a member of the American Institute of Certified Planners, American Planning Association, Planning Accreditation Board, South Florida Planning and Zoning Association, National Association of Cuban Architects, and American Institute of Architects among others. He obtained his bachelor's degree in architecture from the University of Florida (1967) and master's degree in regional planning from the University of North Carolina (1969).

GEORGE ROWE recently retired as Director of Public Works, City of Cincinnati, Ohio. A leader in that city's successful programs to revitalize its public works infrastructure, in 1989 Mr. Rowe was named one of the Top Ten Public Works Leaders of the Year by the American Public Works Association and is 1993 president elect of that organization. He received his B.S. degree in architectural engineering (1950) from the Hampton Institute and completed graduate studies in civil engineering at the University of Cincinnati. A licensed engineer in the state of Ohio and active in professional and civic organizations, Mr. Rowe has served as Vice President of the APWA Research Foundation and member of the Board of Directors of Engineers and Scientists of Cincinnati.

RICHARD L. SIEGLE, P.E. is Director of Facilities Services for the Smithsonian Institution and formerly the Director of Design and Construction for the State of Washington. An officer for more than 20 years with the Navy Civil Engineer Corps, he served in engineering and teaching positions throughout the United States and in the Pacific and Far East. He received his B.S. in civil engineering from the University of Illinois and M.S. in civil engineering from Stanford University. Mr. Siegle is a registered professional engineer, Fellow of the American Society of Civil Engineers, and member of the National Society of Professional Engineers, Association of Physical Plant Administrators, and the American Association of Museums. Mr. Seigle also serves on the design committee of the Pennsylvania Avenue Development Corporation and on the Federal Construction Council of the National Academy of Sciences.

RAYMOND L. STERLING, Ph.D. is Shimizu Professor of Civil and Mineral Engineering, Director of the Underground Space Center, and Associate Professor, University of Minnesota. A registered engineer and active participant in a range of professional organizations, Dr. Sterling is a specialist in the design and construction of underground structures. He received his Bach. Eng. degree (1970) from the University of Sheffield and his M.S. in geological engineering (1975) and Ph.D. in civil engineering (1977) from the University of Minnesota. He is a member and Chairman of the Geotechnical Board's U.S. National Committee on Tunneling Technology.

NAN STOCKHOLM is Director of the Presidio Council, which is developing key concepts and strategies for conversion of the Presidio military post in San Francisco from military use to a unit of the Golden Gate National Recreation Area. Previously, she served as Associate Majority Counsel, Senate Environment and Public Works Committee (1985-1989), and subcommittee counsel for Senator Daniel Patrick Moynihan; Director, Conference of Western Attorneys General; and Counsel, Western Legislative Conference, Council of State Governments (1984-1985). Ms. Stockholm received her A.B. (1976) from Stanford University and the J.D. degree (1981) from Stanford Law School. She is a member of the bars of California and the District of Columbia.

BRB/CETS Liaison

NANCY RUTLEDGE CONNERY is a consultant in public works and infrastructure, and is affiliated with the Taubman Center for State and Local Government at the J.F. Kennedy School of Government at Harvard University. She was the Executive Director, National Council for Public Works Improvement. Ms. Connery received her B.A. in political science from the Pacific Lutheran University and a master is in public administration from Harvard.

BRB Staff

ANDREW C. LEMER, Ph.D., an engineer-economist and planner, is Director of the Building Research Board. He was formerly Division Vice President with PRC Engineering, Inc., and is the founder and President of the MATRIX Group, Inc. He has served as a consultant to the World Bank, the U.S. Department of Transportation, and the National Institute of Building Sciences. Dr. Lemer is a member of the American Institute of Certified Planners, the American Society of Civil Engineers, the Urban Land Institute, and the American Macro-Engineering Society. He received his S.B., S.M., and Ph.D. degrees in civil engineering from the Massachusetts Institute of Technology, and was a Loeb Fellow at Harvard University's Graduate School of Design for 1992-1993.

APPENDIX B

THE BRB/CETS/NRC STRATEGIC PROGRAM IN INFRASTRUCTURE

The Building Research Board (BRB), Transportation Research Board, Water Science and Technology Board, Marine Board, Board on Telecommunications and Computer Applications, and other units of the academy complex[20] have long been involved in studies and research related to infrastructure. Much of this work has focused on particular modes of infrastructure or stages of the service delivery process (e.g., construction), but several studies have aimed to contribute directly to the national discussion of infrastructure systems (see, for example, Ausubel and Herman, 1988). The NRC provided advice to the National Council on Public Works Improvement on matters of technological innovation (NRC, 1987), in the process contributing to the development of a concise definition of "infrastructure" that has subsequently gained some support in professional and policy circles.[21]

THE ACADEMY'S STRATEGIC PROGRAM

Participants in these various NRC activities, particularly members and staff of BRB and its parent unit, the Commission on Engineering and Technical Systems (CETS), began to develop the view that the dearth of consensus or action on infrastructure problems—underinvestment, inadequate maintenance,

---

[20]The National Research Council and its parent bodies, the National Academy of Sciences, National Academy of Engineering, and Institute of Medicine.

[21]For example, the report was one of the first to focus on infrastructure as a stream of services as well as constructed facilities.

lagging technological progress—may be attributed to the public's lack of understanding that the problems exist, that increased attention is warranted by benefits to be gained in relation to other societal needs, and that progress is possible. In this case, NRC observers reasoned, those concerned about the future of the nation's infrastructure need new ideas and ways to overcome the institutional and social barriers to improvements in infrastructure.

CETS undertook in 1988 to formulate a strategic program to foster such new ideas and ways of presenting those ideas. The director and several members of the BRB were assigned responsibility for formulating the program, and subsequently for the program's continuity and leadership. An essential early step was to create simultaneously a visible institutional focus on infrastructure within the academy and a forum to bring together a broad constituency for the program's results. The program was envisioned to address directly both topics related to particular infrastructures and cross-cutting topics not within the scope of current academy activities. For topics related to particular infrastructures within the purview of current academy activities, the program would foster a broad multidisciplinary outlook but would draw primarily on the resources of existing units within the academy complex.

The program as a whole would provide a framework and strategic direction for specific individual activities to be undertaken on a stand-alone basis. Each such activity would be defined through planning within the BRB or other units, perhaps with the participation of a larger group of volunteers and potential sponsors. Sponsorship of symposia, colloquia, committee studies, or other activities would then solicited for each specific activity after approval by the NRC Governing Board.

On this basis, the BRB held a planning meeting in November 1988 in Washington, D.C., which involved staff and members of CETS, BRB, and the other NRC units with major interests related to infrastructure. Besides confirming and extending the initial strategy, this meeting yielded a sharper description of how the NRC might effectively enhance the national infrastructure policy debate: a series of colloquia on specific infrastructure topics would increase the program's exposure and motivate further activities within the NRC and elsewhere. The meeting's participants developed a preliminary listing of specific topic areas on which the CETS/BRB efforts might focus, and identified staff liaisons between the BRB and other interested units within the academy, as well as outside agencies.

A meeting in Cambridge, Massachusetts in September 1989 brought together BRB staff and volunteers and representatives of several federal agencies interested in the program. The participants produced a more detailed definition of promising colloquium topics, including two topics identified as having high priority: (1) facility monitoring and nondestructive evaluation for infrastructure management, and (2) Progress and consequences of large- scale infrastructure deterioration and failure. These results became the basis for a prospectus, approved by the NRC Governing Board in December 1989, for a colloquium series planned for a three-year period.

The lack of clear and comprehensive federal agency responsibility for infrastructure combined with growing budgetary constraints to limit drastically the willingness of potential sponsors to make commitments to the program. By early 1991, BRB had received only a fraction of the support solicited for the colloquium series; this support came from the National Science Foundation and the Department of the Army. However, judging that further delay would severely threaten the strategic program's potential for positive impact, the BRB decided to proceed with the colloquium series. The Committee on Infrastructure, appointed to direct the series and advise on the overall program, held its first meeting on May 23 and 24, 1991.

SCOPE OF THE PRESENT STUDY

As initially defined, the series of colloquia was designed to address topics of immediate interest, substantial payoff in terms of motivating improvements in the nation's infrastructure, and long-term relevance. Each colloquium was meant to serve as a vehicle for motivating further research and action on the topics covered, by bringing together institutions and ideas, and focusing attention on needs, opportunities, and barriers to progress in infrastructure.

In its initial discussions, the committee determined that the topics designated for initial colloquia were unlikely to be very effective in achieving the underlying goals of the program. Reasserting that infrastructure has strategic national importance but that it is nevertheless essentially a local problem, the committee decided that a series of three regional colloquia should be held to explore the elements of success experienced by local governments in addressing their infrastructure problems.

This marked an important departure from the approach pursued in most earlier studies of infrastructure. These earlier studies had focused primarily on one or more modes of infrastructure (e.g., highways, water supply). The committee chose instead to focus on infrastructure as a multimodal system within a region. By comparing how this system has been managed several regions, the committee hoped to gain new insights into the principles and strategies for more effective management of the nation's infrastructure.

The committee concluded that its greatest contribution would be in identifying and describing common and transferable principles and strategies that can be applied in other regions, taking into account both short- and long-term perspectives and possible alternative patterns of future urban development and technology. That conclusion is the source of this report.

OTHER STUDIES

In developing its 1988 report *Fragile Foundations*, the National Council on Public Works Improvement found that none of the various measures available gives a clear, comprehensive, and convincing picture of the status of the nation's infrastructure (NCPWI, 1988). In this, the council echoed the concerns of an earlier body whose 1984 report *Hard Choices* had questioned at length the widely used concept of measurable "need" for infrastructure. These studies exemplify a growing awareness among professionals and policymakers that the ways performance of infrastructures is characterized and the standards used to judge whether performance is acceptable have far-reaching but poorly understood consequences for how problems are perceived and what solutions appear reasonable.

As a part of its efforts to explore appropriate elements of future federal government roles in infrastructure development and management, the Army Corps of Engineers, Institute for Water Resources, undertook (in the early 1990s) to identify and address key issues of infrastructure performance and its cost-effective achievement. Institute staff asked the BRB to plan a colloquium on the topic, with a twofold objective: (1) to develop a list of key issues related to the definition, measurement, and achievement of cost-effective infrastructure performance, and (2) to delineate the principal areas to be explored in addressing these issues in a subsequent NRC study, such as data needs, problems of measurement, problems of institutional structure, and others. Discussions in the colloquium and subsequent study activities will be restricted to issues arising from infrastructure within urban regions. These activities commenced in 1993 and are scheduled to be completed early in 1995.

Recognizing that enhancing the science and technology of infrastructure systems can make a substantial contribution to the nation's productivity and quality of life, National Science Foundation (NSF) undertook (in late 1992) to define new programs for research in these areas. The NSFs Division of Mechanical and Structural Systems of the Directorate of Engineering asked the BRB, in cooperation with the Geotechnical Board, to undertake a study to define the state-of-the-art, basic research needs and priorities related to the structures, geomechanics, and building systems of infrastructure. The resulting research agenda will present high-priority opportunities that may be used by the National Science Foundation and the research community to guide basic infrastructure core research, targeted ultimately to provide lessons of cross-cutting value for effective infrastructure development and management.

The study is focused on fundamental underpinnings of physical infrastructure technology, but it will be shaped by the broad national policy debate reflected in such reports as those by the National Council on Public Works Improvement and others already mentioned. The study will also build on other infrastructure research agenda-setting efforts, including work by organizations such as the Civil Engineering Research Foundation's "National Civil Engineering Research Needs Forum" and the International Society for Arboriculture's "National Research Agenda for Urban Forestry in the 1990s."

THE PROGRAM'S FUTURE

Other activities are being developed within the framework of this strategic program. "Education for Stewardship" refers broadly to several proposals that changes in education are needed, both at the professional level and in primary and secondary schools, to foster more effective interdisciplinary development and management of infrastructure systems and broader appreciation of the important role of infrastructure as a public asset. "Toward Urban Ecostructure" refers to the application of environmentally friendly or advantageous technologies in providing the facilities and services of infrastructure.

The program's achievements to date and a growing level of interest in federal roles in the nation's infrastructure suggest that a more permanent forum for review and discussion of infrastructure may be warranted. CETS members are considering a range of alternative activities that will advance the discussion of infrastructure and action to deal with issues of infrastructure facing the United States.

REFERENCES

Ausubel, J.H., and Herman, R., ed. 1988. Cities and Their Vital Systems: Infrastructure Past, Present, and Future, Washington, D.C.: National Academy Press.

NCPWI (National Council on Public Works Improvement). 1988. Fragile Foundations: A Report on America's Public Works. Washington, D.C.: U.S. Government Printing Office.

NIAC (National Infrastructure Advisory Committee). 1984. Hard Choices. Report to the Joint Economic Committee of the U.S. Congress. Washington, D.C.: Government Printing Office.

NRC (National Research Council). 1987. Infrastructure for the 21st Century: Framework for a Research Agenda, Washington, D.C.: National Academy Press.

APPENDIX C

STUDY PARTICIPANTS

Site Visits and Meeting: Phoenix, Arizona
March 20-21, 1992

Committee on Infrastructure:

Chairman
Albert A. Grant

Members
Claire Barrett
Michael Cohen
Ellis Lane Johnson
Gordon S. Kino
William Rees Morrish
Joseph Perkowski
Janice Elaine Perlman
Sergio Rodriguez
George Rowe
Richard L. Siegle
Raymond L. Sterling
Nan Stockholm

Federal Liaison Representatives
Kyle Schilling, U.S. Army Corps
of Engineers

NRC Liaison Representatives
Nancy Rutledge Connery, Public
Works Infrastructure

Phoenix Public Officials
Todd Bostwick, City of Phoenix
Pueblo Grande Museum
Michael Fifield, College of
Architecture and Environmental
Design
Gretchen Freeman, Phoenix Arts
Commission
Bruce Henning, Public Works
Department
Richard Jaquay, Black and Veatch
Ron Jensen, Public Works
Department
Walt Kinsler, Department of
Parks, Recreation, and Libraries
George Kirk, Sunnyslope Village
Alliance
Mark Lamm, Department of
Parks, Recreation, and Libraries
Dan Lance, Arizona Department
of Transportation
David Longey, Sunnyslope
Village Alliance
David Mahaffey, Black and
Veatch

113

Jim Matteson, Street
  Transportation Department
Joy Mee, Planning Department
Ed Raleigh, Flood Control
  District of Maricopa County
John Rodriguez, Flood Control
  District of Maricopa County
Joan Roberts, North Mountain
  Village Planning Committee,
  Sunnyslope Urban Design
  Committee
Ron Romley, Arizona Department
  of Transportation
Tom Sands, Salt River Project
Jeffrey Sheman, Chairman,
  North Mountain Village
  Planning Committee
Deborah Whitehurst, Phoenix Arts
  Commission

Invited Participants
John Smart, Bureau of
  Reclamation
Catherine Brown, University of
  Minnesota
Janet Felsten
Helene Grant
Sharon Perkowski

BRB Staff
Andrew C. Lemer, Director,
  Building Research Board

**Site Visit and Meeting: Cincinnati, Ohio
June 4-6, 1992**

Committee on Infrastructure

Chairman
Albert A. Grant

Members
Claire Barrett
Ellis Lane Johnson
Gordon S. Kino
William Rees Morrish
Sergio Rodriguez
George Rowe
Richard L. Siegle

**Federal Liaison Representative
to the Committee**
Charles W. Neissner, Federal
  Highway Administration

Public Facilities Council
Elisha C. Freedman, BRB
Russell E. Doeg, Connecticut
Buck Katt, Missouri
Robert Grinch, Ohio
H.P. Anderson, Commonwealth
  of Pennsylvania
Tom Henderson, Capital Budget
  Assistant, Office of Financial
  Management, Washington State
Leo Thomas, Port Authority of
  New York and New Jersey

Invited Participants
Catherine Brown, University of
  Minnesota
J.B. Jones, Acting Principal
  Architect
Robert Richardson, Division of
  Architecture

John Smart, Bureau of
  Reclamation

Speakers/Panelists
John Andreyko, Department of
  Finance
Chaunston Brown, Avondale
  Community Council
Stuart Brown, Department of
  Economic Development
Prem Garg, Division of Sanitation
Scott Johnson, Cincinnati Union
  Terminal
Donald Lewis, Department of
  Law
Jerry Metz, Winton Place Civic
  Club
Ronald F. Meyer, Department of
  Public Works
John Mirlisena, Council Member
Donna Moubray, Hartwell
  Community Council
John Smale, Procter and Gamble
  Company
Bobbie Sterne, Council Member
Thomas Stitt, Consultant
Tyrone Yates, Council Member
Thomas E. Young, City Engineer

BRB Staff
Andrew C. Lemer, Director
Building Research Board

115

**Site Visit and Meeting in
Boston, Massachusetts
August 31, September 1-3, 1992**

Committee on Infrastructure

Chairman
Albert A. Grant

Members
Claire Barrett
Michael Cohen
Ellis Lane Johnson
Gordon S. Kino
David Hunter Marks
William Rees Morrish
Joseph Perkowski
Janice Elaine Perlman
George Rowe
Richard L. Siegle
Raymond L. Sterling

Federal Liaison Representative
Charles W. Neissner, Federal
Highway Administration

NRC Liaison Representative
Nancy Rutledge Connery,
Consultant

BRB Member
Catherine Brown, University of
Minnesota

**Speaker at August 31 Dinner at
St. Botolph Club**
Alex Krieger, Director of Urban
Design, Harvard University

**Presenters at September 1
Breakfast at
Sheraton Boston Hotel**
Fred Salvucci, former Secretary
of Transportation for the
Commonwealth and participant
in Boston Transportation
Planning Review
Tony Pangaro, Southwest
Corridor Project Manager

**Participants in Tour of
Southwest Corridor Subway
Project**
Tony Pangaro, Project Manager
Ken Kruckemeyer, Design
Architect
David Lee, Architect, Ruggles
Station
Ann Hershfang, South End
Community Leader
Edwina Cloherty, Jamaica Plain
Community Leader
Dee Primm, Roxbury Community
Leader
Jacquelyn Hallsmith, Design
Coordinator

**Panel at South Station
Luncheon**
SPEAKER: Richard Taylor,
Secretary of Transportation and
Construction
Peter Zuk, Central Artery Project
Manager

Valerie Southern, Federal
Highway Administration, New
England Region
William Twomey, Consultant
TAMS, previous project
manager Mark Primack,
President, Move Massachusetts
2000 and Executive Director,
Boston GreenSpace Alliance

**Massachusetts Water Resources
Authority Deer Island,
Winthrop**
Douglas MacDonald, Executive
Director
Peter Koff, Attorney for City of
Quincy (original filer of Boston
Harbor law suit)
Julie Belaga, Northeast Regional
Director (EPA)
Peggy Reilly, Town of Winthrop,
Community Participant

BRB Staff
Andrew C. Lemer, Director
Building Research Board

117